Additional Publications
by Victor Kwegyir

The Business You Can Start:
Spotting the Greatest Opportunities in the Economic Downturn
(Pathway to Business Success Series) by Victor Kwegyir

The Business You Can Start Workbook
Creating the Greatest Opportunities for a Successful Business by Victor Kwegyir

Business 365
Daily Inspiration for Creativity, Innovation and Business Success by Victor Kwegyir

Pitch Your Business Like a Pro:
Mastering the Art of Winning Investor Support for Business Success
(Pathway to Business Success Series) by Victor Kwegyir

Beyond the Passion:
What It Takes to Achieve Success in Business
(Pathway to Business Success Series)
by Victor Kwegyir

Quotable Quotes for Business:
Lessons for Success (Pathway to Business Success Series) by Victor Kwegyir

You've Been Fired! Now What?
Seize the Opportunity, Creatively Turn It into a Successful Reality
by Tonia Askins and Victor Kwegyir

OPPORTUNITIES *in the* NEW ECONOMY *and* BEYOND

Birthing Entrepreneurs in a Pandemic Economy to Create Successful Businesses and New Wealth

Victor Kwegyir
Entrepreneur, Business Consultant, Coach & Speaker

OPPORTUNITIES IN THE NEW ECONOMY AND BEYOND

Copyright © 2020 by Victor Kwegyir

All rights reserved. No part of this book may be used, reproduced, stored in a retrieval system or transmitted, in any form or by any means, including mechanical, electronic, photocopy, recording, scanning and methods not invented or in common use at the time of this publication, without the prior written permission of the publisher.

Published by
Vike Springs Publishing Ltd.
www.vikesprings.com

First Edition
ISBN - 978-1-8380718-2-0 – Ebook
ISBN - 978-1-8380718-3-7 - Paperback

PATHWAY TO BUSINESS SUCCESS SERIES

Printed in the United Kingdom
and the United States of America

To request Victor for speaking engagements,
interviews, mentoring, proposal writing, ghost writing and publishing,
coaching or consultation
services, please send an email to:
admin@victorkwegyir.com

Victor's books are available at special discounts when purchased in bulk for promotions or as donations for educational and training purposes.

LIMIT OF LIABILITY/DISCLAIMER OF WARRANTY

This publication is designed to provide accurate and authoritative information in regard to the subject matter covered. It is sold with the understanding that the publisher and author are not engaged in rendering physiological, financial, legal or other licensed services. The publisher and the author make no representations or warranties with respect to the completeness of the contents of this work. If expert assistance or counselling is needed, the services of a specific professional should be sought. Neither the publisher nor the author shall be liable for damages arising here from. The fact that an organisation or website is referred to in this work as a citation and/or a potential source of further information does not mean that the author or the publisher endorses the information that the organisation or website may provide or recommendations it may make, nor does the cited organisation endorse affiliation of any sort to this publication. Also, readers should be aware that due to the ever-changing information from the web, Internet websites and URLs listed in this work may have changed or been removed.

All trademarks or names referenced in this book are the property of their respective owners, and the publisher and author are not associated with any product or vendor mentioned.

DEDICATION

To everyone affected by the pandemic and looking for ways to survive, start new businesses, grow them into successful enterprises to create new wealth. I say to you that it is possible. Stay focussed, work at it and see your dreams become a reality. It might be daunting and take longer than you thought, but it will be worth it for the experience and success.

ACKNOWLEDGEMENT

I am grateful to everyone who has been there for this journey and to everyone who has inspired me with their encouragement and helped me to put this eight publication together. Another exciting resource for aspiring entrepreneurs, entrepreneurs, business owners and especially many who the pandemic has gravely affected and need a way out.

I am always grateful to God for continued mercies, strength, wisdom and ability to do what I do; to my pastor, Pastor Matthew Ashimolowo, President and Senior Pastor of Kingsway International Christian Centre (KICC), for continued inspiration to strive for excellence and explore possibilities to make an impact in our generation; to all my great friends and family who have been a great network of support to me in my journey; Mr & Mrs Wyn Knucles, Michael Ajose, Mrs. Kemba Agard, Mr & Mrs Babatunde, to Pastor Ade D'Almeida – KICC, and to my entire family for their prayers, encouragement and support. You have all contributed in many ways to make this a reality. I appreciate you.

THANK YOU all once again!!!

TABLE OF CONTENTS

Acknowledgement ix

Introduction xiii

1. The Nature Of The New Norm 1

2. Reasons for Optimism 9

3. The Advantage Of Starting In A Downturn 37

4. Benefits of Starting a Business..................................... 47

5. Spotting Ideas and Identifying Opportunities............ 55

6. A Few Business Ideas Worth Checking out............... 75

7. Steps in Developing an Idea... 83

8. Creating a Distinction for Your
Product or Service.. 91

9. Proven Strategies For Growth................................... 101

10. How to Put a Compelling Plan Together............... 131

11. Qualities of Successful Businesspeople 159

12. Conclusion... 167

Appendix I 176

Appendix II 177

Appendix III 178
Appendix IV 179
References 180

INTRODUCTION

This book teaches you everything you need to know about how to spot lucrative business opportunities during periods of global economic downturn and build successful businesses from scratch. It also gives you insider knowledge on how successful multi-billion-dollar businesses began during times of economic downturn – and how they are still thriving.

Over the centuries, the human race has faced one crisis after the other and yet somehow, irrespective of how many lives sadly perished or were adversely affected, we have always come through to the other side.

As an entrepreneur with two thriving businesses with multiples streams of income, a business owner and coach, I know **there is reason to be optimistic**. And that irrespective of the dire nature of the situation, we will once again come through to the other side.

The question will be, to what or with what?

The new coronavirus disease (COVID-19) was first identified in December 2019 in China, and declared a pandemic in March 2020. Its worldwide spread has already had a significant impact on the global economy.

According to the ILO (International Labour Organisation), the world lost nearly 400 million full-time jobs in the second quarter of 2020 due to COVID-19.

In March-April 2020, it was estimated that up to 650,000 employees on payroll lost their jobs in the UK, while according to the US jobs report for April 2020, the country has lost 20.6 million jobs since March 2020.

In the European Union market area, the unemployment rate went up to 6.7% across the Union in May; the highest level for eight months. Job losses in Africa were much more than anticipated while many more working hours were lost in Asia due to the increasing impact of the pandemic.

According to a UN Economic Development report released in April 2020, the ILO also estimates that up to 1.6 billion people employed in the informal economy – or nearly half the global workforce – could see their livelihoods destroyed due to the continued decline in working hours brought on by lockdowns to curb the spread of COVID-19.

On a webinar with medical practitioners from Africa and China in March 2020, Jack Ma, of the Alibaba Group said,

"The virus does not distinguish between race and people. The virus does not need a passport. The virus tells us no matter how strong a country appears to be, we are all weak and fragile in front of this disaster."[1]

In the European Union market area, the unemployment rate went up to 6.7% across the Union in May, the highest level for eight months, but lower than what many economists had predicted. However, others warned that Europe may only have deferred the full impact of the crisis on the labour market due to the furlough scheme which had up to 40 million workers' wage bills picked up by governments while they were at home. As Fabio Panetta, ECB (European Central Bank) executive board member warned in a speech on 1st July 2020, *"the worst of the impact on labour markets may be yet to come. ... Some workers on short-time work scheme may not be able to return to their jobs and hiring looks likely to stay subdued"*.[2]

With the challenges and uncertainties associated with COVID-19, we are expecting significant changes in how we live, even after the pandemic is well under control. **This means more opportunities for entrepreneurs to rise to the occasion with solutions, ideas, tools and services that will help us all adapt to new ways of life.**

The truth about challenging times is that they always birth new entrepreneurs. When one person looks at a situation and cries "OBSTACLE! PROBLEM! IMPOSSIBLE!", another shouts "OPPORTUNITY! POTENTIAL! ADVANTAGE!" It all comes down to perspective. The reality is that whatever the global economy goes through, it ALWAYS BOUNCES BACK. That is how we are wired; to find solutions to problems, and work our way out of dire situations.

This book will:

- Help you identify opportunities the economic downturn presents to entrepreneurs, aspiring entrepreneurs and business owners;
- Help you identify business opportunities and gaps in the market;
- Provide examples of smart entrepreneurs who started businesses in financial crises that have grown into multi-billion-dollar corporations;
- List industries and sectors with the most potential business opportunities that can be started right now, with minimal capital;
- Teach you practical ways to test the economic viability of your business ideas;
- Outline the benefits of going into business for yourself; and
- Provide a step-by-step guide on how to start your business

Whether you are someone who has lost their job, are not sure if you will have one to go back to after the crisis, or if you are an employee or business seeking new opportunities, this book will inspire you to take a second look at the economy, anywhere in the world, and see the rare business opportunities you can take full advantage of.

In this challenging time, there are new entrepreneurs to be birthed, new innovative ideas to be discovered, new businesses to emerge and new wealth to be created. Will you be one of those who will rise to take their place in this new wave? I truly hope I can help you do just that.

THE NATURE OF THE NEW NORM

> *"We cannot re-write the chapters of history already past, but we can learn from them, evolve and adapt. The new normal may even be a better normal, certainly a different normal."*
> Ian Davis, Managing Partner at McKinsey

It is no secret the global economy has been seriously shaken like never before, and is indeed still trembling, to say the least. The nature of this crisis is a once-in-a-generation kind of situation and unfortunately has not left anyone or anything out. According to Jack Ma, of the Alibaba Group, the reality is that *"the virus does not distinguish between race and people. The virus does not need a passport. The virus tells us no matter how strong a country appears to be, we are all weak and fragile in front of this disaster."*[3]

Ian Davis, Managing Partner at McKinsey, in his article 'The New Normal'[4], summarises the current situation this way: *"For some organisations, near-term survival is the only agenda item. Others are peering through the fog of uncertainty, thinking about how to position themselves once the crisis has passed and things return to normal."*

But the question remains, what will this new normal look like? No one is able to say how long this crisis will last, and all we know is that what we will face on the other side will not be what we had before.

Throughout history, recessionary periods have always been quite challenging to navigate, however, they have also acted as a catalyst to inspire entrepreneurs to rise and innovate, creating industry-defining businesses and new wealth over the years. Most of the entrepreneurs and businesses that thrive under these conditions focus on looking out for opportunities to deliver products and services that meet the changing needs of clients and society at the time of the crisis and beyond.

Often during such crisis periods, while many businesses are folding, others are expanding, and developing the capacity to absorb the shocks from the uncertain winds that have blown their way; not to mention the many new businesses that spring up to offer alternative solutions to the challenges created by the new demand in the economy.

That is why it has never been a surprise to me to find stories like the one below, amidst all the negativity being reported daily:

According the Americans for Tax Fairness and the Institute for Policy Studies' Program for Inequality, report[5] based on Forbes data for America's more than 600 billionaires between March 18 and May 19, 2020, the net worth of America's billionaires grew 15% during the two-month period, from $2.948 trillion to $3.382 trillion. The biggest gains were enjoyed by the five richest billionaires – Jeff Bezos, Bill Gates, Mark Zuckerberg, Warren Buffett, and Larry Ellison. They saw a combined wealth gain of $76 billion. With Elon Musk had the largest percentage gain, seeing his net worth jump by 48% in the two months to $36 billion. Mark Zuckerberg saw his wealth surge by 46% to $80 billion. Jeff Bezos' increased by 31% to $147 billion, and his ex-wife, Mackenzie Bezos, also saw her wealth increase by a third, to $48 billion.

Having said that, for the year to date according to Bloomberg Billionaire's Index[6], Warren Buffett's wealth has declined by $20 billion, Bill Gates' is down by $4.3 billion. Jeff Bezos on the other hand gained $35.5 billion while Zuckerberg is up by $9 billion.

What We Are Faced With

Humanity over the years has suffered plagues and pandemics with impacts of varied proportions. In the last century alone, plagues such as the American polio epidemic (1916), Spanish Flu (1918-1920), Asian Flu (1957-1958), AIDs epidemic (1981-present day), H1N1 Swine Flu pandemic (2009-2010), West African Ebola epidemic (2014-2016), Zika Virus epidemic (2015-present day) and now the Coronavirus (December 2019 ongoing).

The new coronavirus disease (COVID-19) is a new illness that affects the lungs and airways. It was first identified in December 2019 in China, and later declared a pandemic on 11 March 2020 by The World Health Organization. COVID-19 spread worldwide with alarming speed, infecting millions of people bringing economic activity around the world to a standstill as countries had to impose tight restrictions on movement to halt it from spreading further. The economic damage is already evident, representing the largest economic shock the world has experienced in this generation.

The impact of COVID-19 has created significant uncertainties in the global economy, with potential multiple waves of infection and corresponding shutdowns and lockdown making it almost impossible to plan anything or even predict its end. The World Bank baseline forecast envisions a 5.2% contraction in global GDP in 2020, despite the extraordinary efforts by governments to address the downturn with physical and monetary support policies. It believes that over the long term, the recession as a result of the downturn will "leave lasting scars through lower investment, an erosion of human capital through lost work and schooling, and fragmentation of global trade and supply linkages"[7].

In the UK, like many other economies around the world, the Bank of England (BOE) had to pump an extra £100bn into the economy in June 2020 to help fight the unprecedented coronavirus-induced downturn. On the 12th of August 2020, the Office for National Statistics revealed UK entered its "largest recession on record", shrinking by 20.4% in the second quarter of the year, sending the economy into its first 'technical recession' since 2009. A crash three times greater than the 2008 financial crisis. In its quarterly report released in August 2020, the BOE warned that part of the UK economy might never recover from the coronavirus, with about a million jobs set to go as GDP plunges to 9.5%, the worst slump in a century.

Make UK, which represents 20,000 of companies of all sizes in the UK conducted a survey[8] of 174 of its members up to July 14th 2020. It found out that the number of companies planning to lay off staff in the next six months rose from 25% to 53% in two months, with almost a third of companies planning to cut between 11-25% of employees, and almost one in ten making between a quarter and half of the work force redundant.

To give us some perspective, let's look at what this comes down to in real terms. It is estimated that one in five jobs in the creative industry in the UK could be lost due to the coronavirus. The Creative Industry Federation warned of a "cultural catastrophe" as a study commissioned by them[9] showed that up to 400,000 jobs could be gone by the end of 2020. This include sectors such as TV, performing arts, architecture, and publishing. Music and theatre have also been badly hit by the halt on live performances, with freelancers across the creative industry particularly at risk with more self-employed roles experiencing more losses.

Policy makers have indicated the jobs market is likely to remain weak for some time with a risk of *"higher and more persistent unemployment"*[10.]

The sad truth is that the significant drop in GDP has far-reaching but uneven consequences. Any significant drop in economic activity will hit areas of the population differently. While some have lost everything, some will feel hardly any impact, and for some it comes with a whole load of uncertainty with no previous example to even draw from.

Business groups and labour unions warns that unemployment will surge as governments wind down the furlough scheme introduced at the start of the crisis to help businesses and employees cope.

As previously mentioned, according to the US jobs report for April 2020 the country lost 20.6 million jobs since March 2020. This has resulted in an unemployment rate of 14.7%, a level not seen since the Great Depression in the 1930s. These figures were more than double the number of job losses seen in the 2007-2009 Great Recession, when 8.7 million Americans lost their jobs. However, before the pandemic, the United States marked a 50-year low unemployment rate of just 3.5% as of February 2020.

The Asian Development Bank's *COVID-19 Economic Impact Assessment Template*[11] calculates the overall impact on 24 developing Asian economies and supplements the findings of the multilateral lender's annual economic publication, Asian Development Outlook – ADO 2020. The template warned that COVID-19 threatens the employment of up to 52.8 million workers in China, while the rest of the region is estimated to lose about 16 million jobs if the pandemic goes on until September 2020, in the "worst case scenario".

Having said that, there is a reason for optimism in the face of the unprecedented challenges ahead.

Part of the reason being that most economies were already more robust than in previous downturns, and as such they are more likely to come around much faster, albeit in a new norm. Just before the pandemic for instance, most of the major economies were reporting some of the lowest unemployment rates in decades, improved GDP growth and had robust physical policies in place.

An EY (Ernst & Young) Item Club report[12] from June 2020 expects the UK economy, for instance, to shrink by 8% this year but believes signs of recovery should start showing up next year. It however warned that the economy will not return to its pre-COVID-19 size until early 2023.

And according to USA Today though, of the total of 20.6 million jobs lost, 18 million are expected to be temporary.

2

REASONS FOR OPTIMISM

> "We are all faced with a series of great opportunities brilliantly disguised as impossible situations."
> Charles R. Swindoll

The challenges and uncertainties associated with the pandemic have resulted in significant changes in how we will live and do things even after the pandemic is well under control. This also means more opportunities for entrepreneurs to rise to the occasion with solutions, ideas, tools and services that help humanity adapt to new way of life.

Having said that, even in the midst of the pandemic, while other businesses have had to close down, adapt or are still finding their way, a number of businesses are actively doing business. A report published by the UK Federation of Small Businesses[13] stated that 8% of small companies launched new products during the pandemic, with 5% expanding the range of services they offer.

A number of businesses have also taken advantage of the situation to strategically expand and grow. For instance, Verizon Communications Inc., bought videoconferencing company Blue Jeans Network Inc. for almost $500 million[14], as an unprecedented number of people worked from home or remotely due to the pandemic, making video conferencing the necessary mode of communication.

Video conferencing tools or software, including GoToMeeting, RingCentral Video, Microsoft Teams, Google Meet, Zoom Meetings, Click Meeting, U Meeting, BigBlueButton, Bluejeans Meetings, Lifesize, Cisco Systems Inc.'s WebEx and Microsoft Corp.'s Skype, and a few others have all become essential as part of the new norm.

This have also led to many other opportunities. For instance, with Zoom's usage exploding from 10 million daily meeting participants in December 2019 to 300 million by the end of April 2020, some security flaws and weaknesses got exposed in its software. This led Zoom to acquire encryption start-up Keybase to help make its video calls more secure. Keybase helped implement end-to-end encryption to protect calls from unwelcome guests (known as Zoom bombing) and clandestine monitoring. It had to freeze development and release of new features and focussed its efforts on a 90-day push to enhance its security. I can personally share an experience where an uninvited guest took over my first webinar on "Opportunities in the Pandemic". It was a very bad experience. Happily, it was solved by this quick move from Zoom.

Here is another interesting story of an organisation and entrepreneur refusing to let go and quickly adapting to the changing landscape to survive the curve while we navigate the season towards recovery. Prior to the pandemic, Ghana-based garment manufacturers African Heritage Clothing (AHC) produced predominantly hospitality uniforms. When COVID-19 hit, the need for such a product disappeared almost overnight. But AHC leveraged the situation to their advantage. Using their existing production facilities and skill-set, they immediately shifted their focus to producing PPE and hospital apparel such as face masks, surgical gowns, scrubs and medical uniforms. According to the founder and CEO, Freddie Shava, a passionate entrepreneur and a firm believer in a 'focused-diversified' business approach, *"we see a big future in the healthcare sector with big funding which is a good case for us; and we are well aware the hospitality sector will bounce back in a big way thus realigning ourselves for a big boost in the future."*

There are many other small, medium and large businesses experiencing growth and expansion even in the lockdown period, including:

Stitch & Story – This online crafts firm with just 11 full-time employees started seven years ago as "Kitchen-table Startup", selling materials and providing tutorials for people who want to learn how to knit and crochet. According to the founders, Jennifer Lam and Jen Hoang, they started the business to inspire a new generation of millennials to learn knitting and crocheting. Lam says, "Sales are surging, up massively. We had an 800% increase in March (2020) alone, compared to the same period last year."[15]

Tone and Sculpt – In January 2019, fitness entrepreneur Krissy Cela launched her app-based workout and nutrition guides as a subscription service, with the aim of creating a worldwide community of like-minded women who wanted to keep in fit and healthy. According to Krissy, "people were very sceptical at first because the traditional way is to go to the gym and hire a trainer." However, this is something that many people can't afford. With gyms closed due to the lockdown, the Tone & Sculpt app reached new levels of popularity. Krissy says, "*We've seen growth of 88% in downloads during April (2020) compared with last year. Turnover has literally tripled in the last year.*" She says her home-based exercise routines are "*helping people to stay on track*" at a time when "a lot of people are finding it difficult even to stay mentally positive".[16]

Reckitt Benckiser, UK and Clorox Company, USA – The makers of the world's top cleaning products have seen significant increases in sales, as we cannot stop sanitizing, bleaching and cleaning every surface and corner of our homes.

Sales in Clorox's cleaning segment (including wipes and bleaches) jumped by 32% in the first quarter of 2020 alone, with overall sales increasing by 15% in the same period.

Sales at Reckitt Benckiser, makers of Lysol and Dettol, saw first-quarter sales increase by 13.5%. In March and April, the sales of aerosol disinfectants jumped by 230.5% and multipurpose cleaners 109.1% on the previous year's sales, according to Nielsen[17].

3M – The producer of personal safety products, including gowns and the N95 respirator masks needed for medical professionals, saw its first quarter revenue grow to $8.08 billion, a nearly 3% increase, bolstered by 21% growth in its health-care segment, and a 4.6% increase in consumer goods such as Scotch-Brite sponges.

Wayfair – This is an e-commerce company that sells furniture and home goods in countries such as the UK,

USA, Canada, and parts of Europe. With more people working from home, Wayfair saw a 20% increase in sales compared to the previous year in the first quarter of the year.

Overstock - Another American company that sells home décor, furniture, bedding and many other goods. It also saw April sales increase by up to 120% compared to the same month in the previous year, with growth occurring in its key home furnishings categories.

Netflix – The many people who found themselves confined due to the lockdown with little to do other than watch television offered a huge boost to media streaming services, such as Netflix. The company saw almost 16 million people create accounts in the first three months of the year, nearly double the number of new sign-ups it saw in the final months of 2019.

In summary the following sectors are some of the best positioned to tap into the pandemic economy: video conferencing platforms, food delivery, logistics and shipping companies, e-learning platforms, biomedical companies, workplace collaboration tools, online media streaming, gaming consoles, grocery stores, Internet service providers, home office furniture retailers, and cyber security companies.

Having said that, existing businesses have a window of opportunity to shake things up:

- Now is the opportune time to invest in and test your online shop and develop it.
- Take advantage of relaxed rules and regulations to see if there are incentives to help make processes much easier and less bureaucratic.
- Explore new ways of working remotely or from home, take advantage of various business grants, schemes, broaden your offerings, etc.
- If you need some major upgrades to your facilities, this is one of the best times to do it.
- With shops and stores empty, maybe it is time to freshen things up around your premises to give your business a fresh look and some TLC.
- Take a look at your workflow and operational systems, potentially engage experts to help you develop a more efficient and effective workflow ready for the new normal.

According to an article by Alara Basul[18], *"COVID-19 sparked a retail transformation in the economy with more than 85,000 businesses launching online stores or joining online marketplaces in the last 4 months"*. According to the article, Growth Intelligence used artificial intelligence to read and interpret millions of business websites across the UK's SME ecosystem and identified the highest number of new e-commerce offerings ever recorded over a four-month period.

Is there a precedent or trend in this?

History has taught us that it is in such crises that fresh, innovative ideas are born as a solution to the challenging times and the new normal.

Most of the billion-dollar businesses out there today were established during the Great Depression or the recessionary years of the 1950s, '70s, '80s, '90s and 2000s.

A few more interesting facts affirm this point. For instance, did you know that:

- Sixteen out of the thirty corporations that make up the current Dow Jones Industrial Average started during a recession?
- **Walt Disney Corporation** began during the recession of 1923-24. During the depression, Walt Disney Productions created cartoons to bring happiness to those suffering from the economic crisis. It was a major success, making around £1.25m during the period. The company became known in people's memories as an outlet

from the struggles of the time. And it is still here with us today.
- In the recession of the early '90s, 25% of the over-forty executives who were made redundant went on to start their own businesses.
- Two of the oldest globally recognised firms, **Proctor & Gamble Co.** and **General Electric Co.**, were founded during the panic and recessionary times of 1837 and 1873, respectively.
- **Burger King** was founded as a franchise restaurant chain during the ten-month recession in 1953.
- **Cable News Network** (CNN) was founded in 1980 during a twenty-two-month recession.
- During the 1979-80 energy crisis, and the subsequent recession between 1981-82, Trip Hawkins, who was then a senior member of the Apple company decided to leave the company and create a new software company. **Electronic Arts** soon became known as a pioneer of the video games industry. Throughout the 1980s, the firm released software and computers, and released their first video game, *Skate or Die*, in 1987. The company has expanded internationally over the last 40 years, with revenue in excess of $5 billion in 2019, employing 10,000 employees in the process.

- **Fedex** Founder Fred Smith developed a concept of a fast and reliable door-to-door delivery service as part of a university project at Yale Business School, at the end of the 1970 recession. After an unimpressive run and struggle to be accepted by the industry, he became known as a pioneer of the modern delivery sector through its tracking service and real-time updates. Fedex's turnover for 2019 was $69.7 billion with 400,000 employees on its books.
- The **Hewlett-Packard** (HP) Corporation began in 1938 during the Great Depression. Stanford Business School alumni, William Hewlett and David Packard created a new electrics company out of a garage in Palo Alto, California – known as Hewlett-Packard. From an initial capital investment of only £435, HP now employs over 65,000 employees and had a turnover of $58.75 billion in 2019.
- **IBM** (International Business Machines Corporation) was created during the 1911 recession in New York where it was known as Computing-Tabulating-Recording Company (CTR). The firm began selling commercial and business machines during the two-year economic downturn and took advantage of the challenging season to set itself apart from the competition as the industry leader. IBM's turnover for 2019 was

$77.14 billion with 352,600 employees on its books.
- **Microsoft Corporation** began during the 1974-75 recession. Bill Gates and Paul Allen, two computer software engineers and childhood friends set up Microsoft. The firm went on to revolutionise the world with its products and services becoming a household name in the process, having introduced so many other products along the way, such as Windows, Office, Xbox, Outlook and many other products and services used by millions worldwide. The company employs 151,163 with a turnover of $125.84 billion in 2019.

It is safe to agree that truly, *"challenging economic times can serve as a motivational boost to individuals who have been laid-off to become their own employers and future job creators,"*[19] says Carl Schramm, president and CEO at Kauffman.

In more recent times some of the new businesses that started in the wake of the 2007-08 financial crisis and immediately after its effect began to hit home include:

PURE GYM (headquarters in Leeds, UK) – Founded in 2009 by Peter Roberts now owned by Leonard Green & Partners. At the end of the 2019 financial year, the company had 263 gyms, 1.1 million members, £255 million turnover, with plans to expand internationally and was set to exchange contracts to acquire Fitness World just before the lockdown.

CROWDCUBE (headquarters in Exeter, UK) Owned by Luke Lang and Darren Westlake, founders of Equity crowdfunding platform. Registered in 2009 but went live in 2011. *"We first began work on Crowdcube right in the middle of the crash. Many people were incredulous that we wanted to start a business that would help to finance high-risk business,"*[20] says Lang. It has 89 staff, an estimated annual revenue of £8.22 million in 2019 with a record of 220 campaigns funded.

MARKET GRAVITY (headquarters in London, UK) – A design consultancy business set up by Gideon Hyde and Peter Sayburn in 2009. Hyde said at the time, *"A recession is a great time for finding talent ... We hired people at about two thirds of the market [salary] rate but we have a profit share model among the team, which appeals to people with an ambitious mindset. There were a lot of people in their mid-twenties who had worked for some good companies but, through no fault of their own, had found themselves out of work."*[21] The company was acquired by 31st May 2017 by Deloitte LLP.

MVF (based in London, UK) – Started by 5 friends in a basement flat. Now employs 500 people, and operates in over 50 countries across the globe, with a turnover of £91.1million in 2019.

There has also been significant increase in **university start-ups** since the financial crash. For instance, Higher Education Statistics Agency research showed that new student start-ups increased by 132% between 2007/8 and 2013/14. Data from Statista showed that in 2007, the Apple Store, for instance, had just 800 apps. This, however, has increased to 1.5million apps, with business apps being the second biggest category, many of which were created by young programmers at universities. Chris Haley, head of start-ups and new technology research at innovation foundation and charity Nesta noted at the time that, "*There's been a big increase in student start-ups since the recession.*"[22]

AIRBNB – Officially founded in August 2008 in San Francisco, California by Brian Chesky, Joe Gebbia and Nathan Blecharczyk. The company started as a way for Chesky and Gebbia to pay their rent, charging about $80 per night to sleep on an air mattress in their San Francisco apartment when local hotels were sold out for a design festival. As the world went deeper into the recession a year down the line, when people felt they were being outpriced by the hotels and leisure industry, they saw an opportunity to expand their business. Total revenue in 2019 was $4.8 billion. According to Forbes[23,] each of the three founders is worth $4.1 billion. According to

Katie Warren of Businessinsider.com, the company was valued at $31 billion in 2019.

GROUPON – Founded by Andrew Manson with headquarters in Chicago Illinois, USA. The business is a website that promotes companies by offering discounts on their products and services to consumers, ever since the middle of the 2008 financial crisis. This helped many retailers better manage the massive fall in business activity during the recession, and fuelled Groupon's rapid growth into a global household name. In an article on FoxBusiness.com March 19 2020 by Audrey Conklin, one of Groupon's first five employees in 2008, now the CEO of experiential marketing platform Surkus, Stephen George, said, *"During a difficult time, Groupon was able to deliver performance-based marketing solutions to connect businesses and brands with their customers. With discounts, incentives and product discovery, Groupon provided a way for companies to get exposure and consumers to ease back into discretionary spending. In times of market uncertainty, technology companies that provide efficiency, cost-savings and transparent value to all parties are the ones that thrive"*[24]. The company's turnover for 2019 was $2.2 billion with close to 43.6 million active customers, according to Statista.com.

CREDIT KARMA – Ken Lin founded personal finance company Credit Karma in the middle of the 2008 recession. The company has its headquarters in San Francisco,

California, USA. *"As the recession took hold, the economy was tough, funding was scarce and there was widespread distrust from consumers,"*[25] Lin told FOX Business. *"I learned in those early days to focus on the long-term. Building and scaling an impactful business requires a drive beyond making money. Having the passion to deliver on your company's purpose will fuel you through the trying times."* The company now has over 100 million users in the United States, UK and Canada, including about half of all U.S. millennials. On February 24 2020, Intuit Inc., the parent company of TurboTax, announced its intention to acquire Credit Karma for $7.1 billion. It further noted that Credit Karma had *"nearly $1 billion in unaudited revenue in calendar year 2019, up 20% from the previous year."*[26]

CLOUDERA – Is an enterprise data cloud company, a US-based Silicon Valley software company founded in 2008 by Google, Yahoo and Facebook engineers, Christophe Bisciglia, Amr Awadallah and Jeff Hammerbacher. The company's total reported revenue was $144.5 million for its fourth quarter of 2019. The company merged with Hortonworks on January 3, 2019. The total revenue for the full fiscal year for the combined company was $479.9 million. The software company and its data warehouse is currently valued at $2.2 billion.

WHATSAPP – Was incorporated in February 2009 with its headquarters in Mountain View California, USA. Former Yahoo executives Jan Koum and Brian

Acton created the encrypted messaging service that enabled people to send messages around the world for free in real-time. The company was acquired by Facebook in February 2014 for approximately $19.3 billion. WhatsApp is world's most popular messaging app, with 1.6 billion active users in 180 countries.

Venmo – Andrew Kortina and Iqram Magdon-Ismail launched digital payment app Venmo, in 2009 as a way for peers to exchange cash digitally without expensive transfer fees. The company was bought by Braintree for $26 million in 2012. PayPal later bought Braintree for $300 million in 2013.

Uber – Uber is an app that connects drivers with riders. The company was founded in 2009 by Travis Kalanick and Garrett Camp. The inspiration came when they both found themselves stuck in Paris on a snowy evening, unable to find a taxi. They asked themselves: "What if you could request a ride simply by tapping your phone?" 'And the rest, as the saying goes, is history.' The company has its headquarters in San Francisco, California, USA, with major offices in London, Sao Paulo, Mexico City and Amsterdam. It also employs over 16,000 people around the world. An Uber ride can be requested in more than 600 cities worldwide, according to the company's website. The rideshare giant has since expanded internationally across various platforms, including food delivery service, a bike and scooter share service and a temporary work staffing service. Uber was estimated to have over 110 million users worldwide.

Slack – This is a work messaging app founded in 2009 by the co-founder of Flickr, Stewart Butterfield. It experienced a significant increase in demand as work from home options became the norm for most organisations. According to the CEO, at the end of the third and fourth quarters of 2019, Slack *"added around 5,000 net new paid customers."*[27] By late March, halfway through the first quarter of 2020, the app "had added 7,000," later crossing the 9,000 mark. Turnover for 2019 was $400.6 million. Slack is valued at $15.9 billion.

Square – Is a merchant services and mobile payment service founded in 2009 by Twitter founder Jack Dorsey and businessman Jim McKelvey. Based in San Francisco, California USA, the company employs about 3,800 employees with an annual turnover of $4.7 billion in 2019. More than 64 million businesses use the technology to facilitate credit card payments and track sales as of mid-2020. The Square app has been downloaded over 33.5 million times by small business that use it to accept credit card payments, track sales and inventory, and obtain finance. By May 2020, the company's market capitalisation was $35.8 billion.

Pinterest – Also headquartered in San Francisco, California USA, Pinterest was founded by Ben Silbermann,

Evan Sharp and Paul Sciarra in 2010. The website and app acts like a digital scrapbook where people can find inspiration and ideas for their interests and hobbies. It is also a visual discovery engine which lets users organise images, links, recipes, and other things. It has over 300 million users, employs 1600 people, and generated over a billion dollars ($1,142.76 million) in revenue in 2019.

Instagram – Mike Krieger and Kevin Systrom created Instagram in 2010, a photo and video sharing social networking service. The site rapidly grew in popularity gaining over a million registered users in the first two months, and up to ten million in a year. It is currently estimated that more than 500 million active users use the platform daily and about a billion every month. They were bought by Facebook in April 2012 for approximately $1 billion in cash and stocks. Annual revenue for 2019 was $14 billion.

These are but a few examples from the millions of new businesses out there that sprung up around the time.

According to Companies House data, in the UK the number of new businesses has risen every year since 2008. In 2015, a record 608,110 companies were set up, this was eclipsed only by 2018-2019 figures, which was 672,890 company incorporations, a year on year increase of 8.5% compared with 2017-2018.

The truth is that the world is the way you want to see it and perspective is everything.

New Businesses Launched During the Pandemic

The COVID-19 pandemic has proven to be no different to the periods I have shared above. Right at the heart of the pandemic, with lockdowns and corporate downsizing, whole industries facing enormous uncertainties and shutdowns, the entrepreneurial spirit of humanity is yet again awakened. We are rising to take on the challenge of providing solutions to meet the needs of the new normal.

Here are a few of the many businesses already launched and actively doing business locally, nationally and internationally. They include:

Boz42 – a date night subscription service. Caroline and her partner Jade decided to launch a date night subscription box after realising the impact of the lockdown on their relationship. The couple were getting restless and frustrated a month into the lockdown and decided to make efforts to spend quality time together. This led to the compiling of a list of indoor date ideas, giving them a first hint into a gap in the market.

Lockdown Presents – Another couple, Simone Girardeau and Steffen Hoyemsvoll launched their business inspired by a family Zoom call to celebrate Steffen's grandma's birthday. The platform connects professional musicians and singers with private audiences for intimate mini concerts via video conference. Users can book classical, jazz, rock, pop or opera musicians to perform, creating a unique experience for their loved ones.

Blaqbase – Founded by Benedicta, Banga is a marketplace designed to support black-owned businesses, due to her frustration at not being able to easily find products such as hair and makeup in her local area. She felt it limited her ability to support these brands, and she also came to realise that black women were the least funded demographic in business. She decided to create a place to make high-quality brands by black women visible. The app also includes a "brand discovery" feature that enables users to learn about new businesses.

Lanes London – Stylist Emma Lane founded the business to make tie-dye tops during the lockdown after her full-time work suddenly came to an end. She honed her previous experience of making six tie-dye tracksuits for her friend's Glastonbury hen do. In an interview for Metro.co.uk, Emma said, *"It just kind of happened. It wasn't like I made a business plan. I bought 15 tops and just thought I'd tie dye them and see if anyone wants them."*[28] It wasn't long before people were messaging her about her garments asking how they could get their hands on them. She launched her Lanes London shop not long after that.

Findbakers – Yasmin Sidat from Lancashire, inspired by the pandemic, was energised to speed up the process of building and launching her business idea. Findbakers is simply a marketplace which gives home bakers the tools to sell their products online and for buyers to shop locally for their sweet treats. Both home bakers and independent bakeries are able to join the platform. It is also free to join. The platform only takes fees from items sold through the platform. This is *"a platform built on the value to bring together all walks of life through a shared love of baking"*[29].

Rosa Floral – Katie Shaw, a fashion stylist who also saw her work come to standstill due to the pandemic, became one of the many who turned their talents into homegrown businesses. It started when she painted botanical watercolour illustrations to relieve her anxiety brought on by the pandemic. She started taking commissions from friends who wanted to bring a bit of the outdoors into their homes in a time when being in nature was limited. Some asked for paintings to be sent to love ones, prompting her to set up her online shop.

Ashdown Organics – Oliver Loveday is a 39-year-old freelancer in the travel industry who was left without any income during the lockdown. He started working for the supermarket chain ASDA (owned by Walmart, USA) on a temporary basis as a delivery driver. This sparked the idea of his own business delivering organic fruit and vegetable boxes. It all came together when a friend who was self-isolating couldn't get to the shops or get any home delivery slots from the supermarkets. One of his friends asked if he could deliver some supplies to them, he asked a few other people and found about half a dozen people who needed food delivery services. Living near a couple of farm shops came in handy. Within 3 weeks, word of mouth had spread and he was arranging 40 deliveries per week. This soon rose to 70, inspiring him to launch his own website to help him run the business.

Pembrokeshire Moments – Rachel Mullett, 61, launched her new business during the lockdown. For the past eight years, she has sold souvenirs wholesale to shops, galleries and cafes in her local town, Pembrokeshire in Wales. With business quickly drying up during the lockdown with no tourist in sight, she said, *"I saw lockdown as an opportunity to re-evaluate and take some training."*[30] She launched photography workshops under the Pembrokeshire Moments banner, offering courses online via video. She has gone ahead to take bookings for a photography tour of the area once restrictions are eased.

ClearWater Hygiene – At the start of the UK lockdown, Andrew and Rachel Montague, a UK based couple, founded the business to make high grade hand sanitisers aimed at frontline workers and the wider public. Twelve weeks into their business, the company has secured for itself an expected contract value of almost £30 million (some of which are multi-year agreements) after securing corporate contracts to supply their products to Post Office, JD plc, BP, Aldi, O2 Retail and others. The company began trading in March 2020 and by July had the capacity to produce 900,000 litres of its products every week. The sanitisers with 80% ethanol liquid are produced at Deeside Gin Distillery in Banchory, Aberdeenshire and bottled in Preston, Lancashire in the UK.

I am personally of the view that a new economy is emerging from this pandemic season. Historical records indicate a trend of more people starting new businesses during recessionary times than any other period. And many such businesses survive, with some growing to become corporate giants.

A lot of this new economy will be heavily influenced by greater reliance on technology including artificial intelligence (AI). I believe the issue of climate change is not far from driving the agenda, especially since a lot of what the climate change lobbyists were calling for seems to have been tested by the nature of this pandemic. Although technology and AI have been part of how we get things done for some time now, it is going to take the centre stage in almost every aspect of our lives, even in sectors we never imagined.

This is one key area any business-minded person, government, or head of intuition should begin to give more thought and consideration to than ever before. The reality is that the change makers are already figuring it out as I write. This season, like others in the past, is due to birth a new breed of entrepreneurs and change-makers.

Having said that, and to keep our focus, it is critical to appreciate that the pandemic has inadvertently highlighted some major things we can consider and take advantage of wherever possible.

To fully participate in the new norm, it is critical to decide to see things differently and take advantage of what is there with less time to worry or cry about what is not there.

Orison Swett Marden, an American writer and a successful hotelier, once made a statement affirming this fact. He said, *"Don't wait for extraordinary opportunities. Seize common occasions and make them great. Weak men wait for opportunities; strong men make them."*

This book is about helping you look at things and situations around you differently, especially in the midst of the economic downturn and uncertainty. It will help you creatively identify business opportunities and equip you with all the necessary tools and steps to create a way out of the uncertainties, just like those making it in the current economic environment – and even better. I believe the way forward for many of us is starting out towards the dreams we have been nursing so long in our minds and hearts, and turning them into money-making ventures. Someone once said, *"Even when opportunity knocks, a man still has to get up off his seat and open the door."*

I believe for many in the current economic atmosphere, it is the time to boldly take a step, look up, and do something, knowing that with determination and relevant knowledge, such as what this book offers you, only the sky is the limit. Or you can crawl into your shell and weep, potentially becoming part of the statistics or wasting away in the process.

As a personal principle, I strongly believe crying over spilt milk is a waste of precious time and energy, be it losing a job or being uncertain of your current source of income. Instead of worrying and weeping, why not find a way of getting hold of another bottle of milk to use? Most of us unfortunately have lost sight of the fact that, as Alexander Graham Bell said, *"When one door closes, another opens; but we often look so long and so regretfully upon the closed door that we do not see the one which has opened for us."*

3

THE ADVANTAGE OF STARTING IN A DOWNTURN

Of course, there are times when conditions may seemingly present themselves as more favourable for a new business start-up. At the same time, the strength of your conviction and passion can make you ride the storms well enough to safety, should you be determined enough and be willing to make the needed adjustments on the way. Napoleon Hill once said, *"The majority of men meet with failure because of their lack of persistence in creating new plans to take the place of those which fail"*[31].

I think we have established in previous chapters that all the facts clearly support the argument that economic downturn is not necessarily a barrier to starting a new business. Instead it brings with it opportune conditions, which, when exploited, can be a great platform for the start and growth of a business:

1. The great PAUSE – Suddenly, we have all been forced to hit the brakes on our hectic flow. This has afforded many people who potentially felt stuck in the ever-moving system without any controls due to the fast-paced nature of 21st century life, an opportunity to take a critical break, re-valuate ourselves for recalibration. It is out of these rare situations that many have been able to look at life and situations differently to birth new ideas and get on course to create new wealth.

   Businesses that felt the need to constantly keep pursuing to compete or lose their ground and market share, also have this singular opportunity to pause and re-evaluate their direction, strategy, skill set, market, technology, etc. All of which are catalysts for innovation and creativity.

2. It is an opportunity for a new business to find its feet, allowing it to test its operational systems. By the time the economy picks up and generated sales start to increase, the systems and knowledge will have been adjusted to operations and can cope with customer requirements efficiently. In other words, if your business can thrive in a

recession, think how it will soar when the good times come again.

3. Levelled Playing Field – The above has also led to the levelling of the "playing field", offering an opportunity for a fresh start for many individuals and organisations. With the shake-up of the economy, some businesses will be able to weather the storm if the fundamentals are in place and they have been adapting over time. Unfortunately, others will fall through the cracks, while others will be brought down to the basics, forcing them to start building again from the bottom. This will afford many the opportunity to rebuild again, hopefully more strategically. For instance, a lot of industries which were finding it difficult to even consider going online or even allowing its employees to work from home, have no choice now, as everyone, including their competitors, are all forced to do the same.

4. Gap and capacity – As competitors and potential competitors lose out and big businesses fall through the cracks, a lot of room is created for new entrants to rise up to fill the gaps left by these collapsed organisations. According to the Centre for Retails research, in the UK alone, 49 companies with 3,140 stores and a combined work force of 61,320 went into administration

by the 5th August 2020. These include Laura Ashley, Brighthouse, Lombok, Kikki.K, Beales, M&Co, DW Sports, Soletrader, Feather & Black, Muji, Cardinal, Peter Jones (China), Harveys Furniture, T M Lewin, Bertram Books, and many more. Sadly, these numbers are potentially going to increase, even though governments are offering a significant number of incentives to keep businesses afloat through this season, which we do not know when it will end.

5. Your potential competitors are weakened, maybe closing up or even selling out, which may also be due to early retirement. You may find an opportunity to slip into if a hole is developing in the marketplace. However, you will need to do extensive market research to test the survival of your product because the economy will eventually recover.

6. Prices often drop during a downturn. This is the right time for fantastic deals in virtually every category, from office furniture to office supplies, land and equipment to personnel and labour. Most asset prices have been knocked down, from real estate to financial markets or even heavy equipment and construction machinery.

7. You can hire more and better-qualified people. When all the giants are laying off staff, you can find great resources at affordable rates. Do you want to form a professional services firm or simply hire a more qualified accountant? There are many professionals (e.g., lawyers, accountants, engineers, IT professionals, bankers, investment advisors) laid off needing a new firm to work for, most of whom are ready to take the job at much lower pay rate.

8. You can buy everything you need at auction. A lot of repossessions mean large equipment, office furnishings and space, restaurant equipment, and other usually expensive large items are on offer at rock-bottom prices. For instance, you could get great deals on fleets of vehicles and trucks for a delivery service or haulage or construction company.

9. Most businesses are looking to change suppliers. Even if your prices are higher, you can offer greater value. There is the advantage of being the new kid on the block when it comes to pitching your products and services. Many companies are desperate to find new partnerships with new companies that have a different, better, or more innovative way of delivering those products and services.

10. Most people, family and friends alike, may be a bit wary or even scared to invest more money into stock or other investments. They may be willing to finance a portion of your new venture or the expansion of an enterprise that has proven itself over time. The main benefit is that they know you and have a relationship with you. Having a solid and competitive business plan that delivers real numbers stands the chance of attracting the capital you need.

11. Most suppliers are giving better credit as they seek new opportunities. Credit markets are still shaky to say the least and some have virtually shut down; the B2B (Business-to-Business) credit flows are keeping money circulating out of sheer necessity. The main advantage is that all parties have more incentive than ever for finding true win-win situations that allow for cash and stock flow. When everyone is looking to survive, great deals can be executed.

12. You can get good PR by showing you are going against the trend, such as some of the examples shared on previous chapters. The media loves aberrations, and if you are optimistic by expanding or getting into business now, you would be in that category. That means you can generate

some great PR by demonstrating your "alternative" view of the market.

13. You can find great "low money" or "no money" down deals. By simply being aware of good opportunities others have overlooked and finding deals, you could get an entire business simply by taking over a lease (along with all the equipment). Many business owners want out at any cost, meaning you can negotiate great win-win deals that allow the current owners an escape while giving you an opportunity to turn around what could be, if run right, a very viable business.

14. In recent times, with the unstable economic situation around the world, a lot of government policies have been put into place to favour the establishment of small businesses. From the US to South Africa, governments are frantically establishing measures such as making soft loans, grants, and tax breaks available to small and upcoming businesses to help curb the high rate of unemployment. Stringent regulatory requirements are even relaxed at times to encourage job creation. There is, therefore, a lot of support to ease the initial hurdles when it comes to stepping out into business.

15. You might have lost your job and have to do something. Sometimes, the best business decision is the one you are forced into, and the incentive as well as the need for income is often enough to push those previously "on the fence" to strike out on their own. In the words of Joseph Campbell, an American writer and lecturer, *"Opportunities to find deeper powers within ourselves come when life seems most challenging."*[32] There is nothing wrong with being in this position; it simply means there is greater urgency to do something that will start to generate income as quickly as possible.

Alvin Toffler, an American writer and futurist and once an associate editor of *Fortune* magazine, once said, *"To think that the new economy is over is like somebody in London in 1830 saying the entire industrial revolution is over because some textile manufacturers in Manchester went broke."*[33]

In conclusion, *"You are surrounded by simple, obvious solutions that can dramatically increase your income, power, influence and success. The problem is, you just don't see them,"*[34] said Jay Abraham. Open your eyes, decide to look at things differently, determine to start something, and make a smart and informed move toward one kind of business or the other. With the right practical steps, you will get hold of your dreams and turn them into reality. *"Don't wait until everything is just right. It will never be perfect. There will always be challenges, obstacles and less than perfect conditions. So what? Get started now. With each step you take, you will grow stronger and stronger, more and more self-confident and more and more successful,"*[35] said Mark Victor Hansen.

Read on as I help you make one good choice after the other in starting the business of your dreams and increasing your earning power and scope of influence.

4

BENEFITS OF STARTING A BUSINESS

Understanding the benefits of entrepreneurship should encourage you in acting out your dream. Although it might seem a bit scary to just think of it at first, especially if you have been used to a well set daily structure of waking up at a set time to rush for the usual 9-5 job, there are really good reasons why starting your own business makes sense.

Just like yourself, many people including me, rather than giving up, chose to take this seemingly unpredictable option to become an entrepreneur. The path I chose led me on a unique journey that has helped me discover my potential. I have since gone on to start another business as I help many others on this entrepreneurial journey. At the time of writing, I have two businesses with multiple streams of income under them, and I look forward to getting a few more ideas off the ground strategically soon.

Although a few specific benefits may differ slightly from community to community or nation to nation, some of the most compelling benefits are as follows:

1. **You are your own boss** – You get to be in control. The demands of having to stick to certain routines and procedures, and even forcing yourself to work with colleagues you cannot get on with, are no more. You can direct your business the way you want it, in line with your dreams and passions. You control and influence every aspect such as the best hiring process, the personality and skills of the employees you are comfortable working with, working hours, management style, and other factors that determine how the business operates.

2. **Learning opportunities** – As a new business owner you often find yourself managing all aspects of the business by yourself. These offer huge opportunities to learn and gain operational knowledge and understanding on all aspects of business functions. In the process, you even discover aspects of yourself that you never thought existed.

3. **The opportunity to challenge yourself** – Following closely from the above, especially if you are not a routine kind of person, you can

be sure that each day as an entrepreneur will be filled with new opportunities to challenge yourself, be creative and learn something new.

4. **You have personal time** – You get to manage your time to suit your personal life and have better control of the work/life balance. For instance, you can plan around your child's daily school runs, your favourite community activities, hobbies, holidays, and other activities that are dear to your heart.

5. **You have unlimited income potential** – You have no limit on the amount of income you earn, and you can pace the growth of your income according to your capacity to produce. The possibility of making more money progressively through your own business, rather than by working for someone else, is more obtainable.

6. **You have flexibility** – Flexibility allows you to make decisions faster, change course or adapt quickly to new opportunities without anyone else's approval. There is therefore no need to feed ideas up any chain of command.

7. **You can set your own goals** – There is no limit to how successful you want to become. Your ambitions are limited only by your own

desires. You can remain in a small business capacity or expand beyond your immediate environs.

8. **Personal satisfaction and creative freedom** – With most entrepreneurs often starting off in what they are passionate about, you are able to direct your energies and creativity in ways that give you the greatest satisfaction, from implementing your ideas, and engaging with clients directly as you see your business grow.

9. **You can impact society** – You can create wealth and use it as you wish to influence society. In the words of Cullen Hightower, *"A true measure of your worth includes all the benefits others have gained from your success."*[36] Running your own business is your best bet in achieving this.

10. **You have reduced personal liability**, especially in the case of setting up as a Limited Liability Company. Many national governments have formally embraced the potential of the creation of small businesses and are vigorously enacting legislations daily, favouring such business owners, for the Sole Proprietor as well as the private Limited Liability Company. Your personal assets are protected against possible company liability.

11. **You can pass on a legacy.** Businesses, in many instances, are deemed separate entities from their owners and directors and have a perpetual existence. They can therefore be passed on to your children, whereas you cannot do this with a job.

12. **You control your destiny.** By having your own business, you have a sense of ownership and destiny, and can have a better life as the business pays for these benefits. This provides a keen sense of purpose.

13. **You have reduced tax liability** – Some expenses you would have paid from a salary can be allocated as business expenses. For instance, as a business grows, the business can buy cars, properties, etc, for the use of its directors, and expenses are charged to the business accounts.

14. **You can have lifetime income –** Your company can generate perpetual income even after retirement.

15. **You are a lifetime employer** – Owning a business gives you an opportunity to be an employer for life, thus positively influencing the lives of others. As an employer, you help your

community and nation deal with unemployment while potentially providing employment for individuals and families.

16. **You can support your cause of choice** – Through your company, you can give to the cause of your choice (charities, educational institutions, etc.). For those who are passionate about charitable causes, no joy compares to setting up your own business and generating the income to fund your vision or support others in theirs.

17. **You have job security** – You are relieved of the thought of ever being "fired". The challenge is to ensure that your business runs profitably and smoothly.

18. **You feel personal achievement** – The joy derived from creating and running a successful business can be exhilarating. As your business grows, the satisfaction of knowing that you did it from the ground up is far more fulfilling than building someone else's business.

19. **You are a problem solver** – As a business owner, your products or services provide solutions for your clients and society at large. As a solution provider, you earn respect in your community and nation.

All said and done, you owe it to yourself to take advantage of the immense benefits you stand to gain in starting your own business. It provides the opportunity to launch, and with the right idea, knowledge, determination, and passion; you will succeed, irrespective of your circumstances. Being your own boss helps you to react faster to opportunities and to grow a business with your own signature and develop positive relationships with clients and staff.

5

SPOTTING IDEAS AND IDENTIFYING OPPORTUNITIES

> *"Capital isn't that important in business. Experience isn't that important. You can get both of these things. What is important are ideas."*
> Harvey S. Firestone, *founder of Firestone Tire and Rubber Company*

You have made that all-important decision to start a business. Some of you might already have a kind of business in mind at this stage, while others have yet to decide on a particular line of business. Whatever stage you are at, this chapter will help you fine-tune and clearly define what kind of business will be best for you.

Before we go any further, let me state this fact: **if you believe you're incapable of coming up with ideas then you won't come up with any.** You will need to put aside any negativity about yourself and your capacity to be creative. Ideas can come from anywhere, and some of the best ideas will seem quite unrealistic or impossible based on your current knowledge, experience, and assumptions.

Honestly, there is no formula when it comes to identifying business opportunities. Being creative in your thinking, closely observing situations and scenarios, and asking the right questions are some of the best ways to start. **Money-making, winning ideas are all around us; a little desire to change your circumstance, a little action, a little patience to wait when you must, a little focus, and engagement with life, and you are buzzing with one.**

In the words of Brian Tracy, a self-help author, *"A major stimulant to creative thinking is focused questions. There is something about a well-worded question that often penetrates to the heart of the matter and triggers new ideas and insights."*[37] On the other hand, Martha Stewart, an American business magnate, TV host, author, and magazine publisher with an estimated net worth of about $628 million in 2019, gave us a little peek into her thinking, saying, *"I'm not a sponge exactly, but I find that something I look at is a great opportunity for ideas."*[38]

Having said that, there are many ideas already out there that need great improvement to meet the growing needs of consumers. To Michael Eisner, former CEO of The Walt Disney Company, *"There is no good idea that can't be improved on."*[39] Different cultures, weather conditions, taste, fashion, habits, and regulations from one nation – and even continent – to the other requires improving on such ideas to adapt to the new environment.

Let us now explore some of the ways we can stimulate our minds to identify business opportunities and ideas to take advantage of.

Turn your hobby into a viable business. This is where you find creative ways of making money out of your hobby, just like in some of the entrepreneurial stories in previous chapters. Someone may be willing to pay for it. Basing your business idea around something you enjoy doing is one of the surest ways of succeeding. Passion and enthusiasm sells better than just introducing a product. Check out my book *Beyond The Passion* for more on this.

Use existing skills from past employment. This is where we challenge you to use your skills and experience that you acquired while working in your current or previous employment to meet the needs of a niche market. You may be able to provide a product or service being sourced by your current place of employment better than a current supplier, become an expert consultant in your industry, or even a trainer in your industry.

Use your personality for a business idea. You could be a good communicator, which suggests being a good salesperson, you could be an outstanding networker, you could be a person who makes everyone feel at home anytime anywhere, or you could be a collector, selling products online to a niche market. All these can give you a fair idea of what to do and where to start from.

Have a closer look at current social trends. Analysing social trends could help you spot an underlying opportunity to explore. For example, more people tend to marry later than ever before, so there are a lot more single parents, fashion trends, behaviours, etc.

It is estimated for instance that up to 1.5 million people are added to the global urban population every week, with up to 90% of this urban population growth taking place in Africa and Asia. Such trends present significant opportunities with vast potential for emerging cities to act as hubs for inclusive economic development, especially when 85% of global GDP is generated in cities[40]. The fact is that urban consumers often tend to be more daring, liberal, tolerant, experienced, and prone to trying out new products and services. Entrepreneurs and business owners are therefore encouraged to go for products, services, experiences or campaigns that are tailored to the very specific needs of urbanites worldwide, if not city by city.

According to TrendWatching.com five key emerging consumer trends, with each one *"presenting a powerful opportunity to build new products, services, campaigns, brands and more that people will love in 2020 and beyond, include:*

1. GREEN PRESSURE

2. BRAND AVATARS

3. METAMORPHIC DESIGN

4. THE BURNOUT.

5. CIVIL MEDIA ."

It is important to appreciate that trends are only useful if you use them to make what you do and the world a better place. Think about them, evaluate the potential opportunities that come with each one of them, and use them to bring about the change you desire.

On the other hand according to Mintel, a leading marketing intelligence agency, the following seven core drivers of consumer behaviour that will shape global markets over the next ten years, are:

1. "WELLBEING – Seeking physical and mental wellness.
2. SURROUNDINGS – Feeling connected to the external environment.
3. TECHNOLOGY – Finding solutions through technology in the physical and digital worlds.
4. RIGHTS – Feeling respected, protected, and supported.
5. IDENTITY – Understanding and expressing oneself and one's place in society.
6. VALUE – Finding tangible, measurable benefits from investments.
7. EXPERIENCES – Seeking and discovering stimulation."[41]

Other major trends to look at include new technologies such as artificial intelligence (AI), telehealth, and robotics. There is a strong demand for digital health technologies – including finding doctors and making appointments online, consulting with doctors by phone and video calls, completing paperwork online before actual appointments, etc.

Another trend is privacy in cashless society; the future will require various tools and products to help protect the consumers' information online.

Another website with some great trends to consider is:

https://www.researchworld.com/top-10-global-consumer-trends-2020/.

Provide services that make others feel good. Some services could help people simplify and de-clutter their lives, at the same time helping them give back to their communities. A business idea to illustrate this is "a junk clearance service," where goods collected are given to charity. You can check out such websites as www.anyjunk.co.uk for more details.

Take advantage of current trends. Consumer attitudes are changing regularly. This is largely influenced by a range of factors such as current fashion, the media, advertising, and demographics. These changes often lead to great business ideas and, in recent years, lifestyle consultants, raw food cafés, and juice bars, to name just a few, have all provided opportunities for entrepreneurs. For instance, talk about obesity, even among children, and the way food is produced has attracted some attention. People are becoming more interested in naturally produced foods, and tracing what they eat back to the source of supply, such as farmers' markets. Some people have become suspicious of traditional medicine and are turning to complementary therapies such as aromatherapy or homeopathy. Have a look at www.trendwatching.com for more inspiration.

Become a tour guide or set up a leisure business in your area. For instance, open a tea shop in an area with high population of pensioners or in one that has a high influx of tourists. Open an outdoor centre in a rural area. Talking to your local council, tourist board, Regional Development Agencies (RDAs), or municipal assembly may give you an idea of priority areas they might already have identified due to research, policy focus, etc.

Explore the possibility of using the latest technology to create a business. The lifestyle of the 21st century thrives much on technology, and there seems to be no end to new ones popping up each day. Facebook, Instagram, Pinterest, Uber, and Twitter, to name a few, are examples of these.

Look into your backyard. Identify problems and difficulties you have experienced in getting things for your home, work, or in your leisure activities.

- Is there any service you need that is not available locally?
- Is there any part of a product that is almost impossible to obtain locally?
- Are there any issues that attract complaints from your neighbours, friends, and even visitors to your locality?
- Are there any problems that cause you inconvenience and are costly to solve?

Ask questions. Listen to people's problems, hopes, dreams, and aspirations. There are often good business opportunities in solving the challenges people face in their businesses or jobs.

Sell other people's goods. It's a known fact that many new firms start off by selling goods that somebody else produced. There are a lot of opportunities to distribute foreign goods in any given country. Distributors are being sought all the time, with the advent of direct marketing. For example, the US Department of Commerce publishes a regular magazine listing businesses looking for facilities and distributors (this is available from all US embassies and consulates). Chambers of commerce and other trade bodies around the world also publish regular listings of businesses seeking partners willing to manufacture under licence or to act as sole distributors.

Research local authorities, large firms, and other public bodies in your area. Get to know what they make and components of their raw materials that they buy from outside the area and see if you can supply such components. You can check out www.direct.gov.uk and www.usa.gov to locate the contact details of your local council or government. More recently, a lot more websites are being created by local and municipal assemblies publishing budget plans and general operational policies, which are all a great source for business ideas.

Look out for potential labour shortages in your area or even overseas. Pursuit of academic qualifications outside of the more traditional vocational training has left many skill shortages in traditional trades. Many office workers and professionals have retrained as plumbers, mechanics, etc, and started their own businesses because of the shortages and the financial rewards that come with it. You could investigate your area for any such possible skill shortages.

Identify opportunities by watching the news. Newspapers, magazines, online discussion forums, blogs, and e-zines are all fruitful sources of new and emerging trends and problems that need a solution. Small advertisement sections of local papers are a good way to get an idea of local patterns of supply and demand. Read the business opportunities sections in the national and local newspapers. Eli Broad, an American philanthropist and founder of Kaufman & Broad (now KB Home) and financial giant SunAmerica (now a subsidiary of AIG) once said, *"There is no substitute for knowledge. To this day, I read three newspapers a day. It is impossible to read a paper without being exposed to ideas. And ideas... more than money... are the real currency for success."* [42] The following resources could be helpful:

- Newspapers and magazines in your country of residence: www.mediauk.com

- Online discussion forums: www.ukbusinessforums.co.uk
- E-zines from around the world: www.ezinearticles.com

Copy business ideas that have taken off elsewhere. A lot of business ideas originate from abroad and get established locally. You can pick up on a trend and be the first to offer that product or service in your local area. For example, the founder of Kwik-Fit, Tom Farmer, got the idea from the "muffler shops" he saw on a visit to the US. The decline in the popularity of DIY led to entrepreneurs in London offering a niche service assembling flat-pack furniture for customers. Websites like www.handylocals.com may help you.

Keep up with changes in the laws of the land. New policies and legislations are often a rich source of new business ideas. They always generate opportunities in terms of administration and implementation. New safety or health regulation requirements may prompt the supply of parts to adapt an existing process to meet the standards, or a demand for people to provide a newly introduced service. For example, the introduction of the new Home Information Packs for buyers and sellers of domestic properties from June 2007 in the UK got people training for the Home Inspector qualification, which qualified them to carry out inspections for the Energy Performance Certificate and the voluntary

Home Condition Report. Keep track of legislation from parliaments and legislative bodies locally, nationally, and around the world for information on new legislation. For examples, visit www.opsi.gov.uk and www.us.gov.

Buy an existing business. However, it's essential to find out why the owner is selling, even if he or she is retiring. Local papers and relevant trade magazines usually advertise businesses for sale. The following sources regularly advertise updated business opportunities: www.daltonsbusiness.com.

Go into franchising. You get the independence and satisfaction of running your own venture but benefit from marketing support and an established customer base. The following web links provide more information and opportunity listings for franchising:
- www.franchiseexpo.co.uk,
- www.thebfa.org,
- www.whichfranchise.com.

Identify products and services to export Look out for products or services that are working in your current city or country of residence and export to other countries that lack such products or services.

Use all the research tools you can find. Surveys, consumer market research, and government statistics are all available online and are easily accessible. On the World

Wide Web are ideas that you can search and explore. You could also get to know of gaps in the market and useful network opportunities. Most local libraries have countless information on this.

Visit exhibitions and trade shows. Major exhibitions are usually packed full of start-up ideas, mostly aimed at people who are seeking to become self-employed. Check:
- www.exhibitions.co.uk,
- www.eventseye.com,
- www.expocentral.com for shows across the globe.

Work as a freelancer. Many more people are choosing to work flexibly from home or outside the traditional employment system. As a freelancer, you can often choose to work from home or in various places to cover absent staff or to help with the peaks and troughs in established businesses. Some professional and experienced managers have set up businesses as an interim, working on short-term assignments or projects at other firms. The variety and flexibility associated with this approach to work keeps attracting more people. Check out information and job listings for freelancers at:
- www.freelancers.net,
- www.fiverr.com,
- www.upwork.com and
- www.freelanceuk.com.

Invent something. Every year, around 20,000 people in the UK apply for patents, with 20% of these applications made by individuals rather than businesses or institutions. Many of today's household names are the brainchild of enthusiastic individuals. Inventions from penicillin to the train all have their roots from the UK. You could get more information from the UK, USA, EU and other Intellectual Property Offices around the world by visiting:

- www.ipo.gov.uk,
- www.uspto.gov,
- www.ec.europa.eu/internal_market/copyright,
- www.wipo.int, and www.patentlawlinks.com.

There are companies that can also help you develop your inventions. My advice is to thoroughly research the best and get good protection and agreements before you make your idea known to them.

Cash in on the 'time poor.' You could start a business that meets the needs of professional and busy people who have little time to themselves. Many kinds of business ideas fall under this category, from simple ones such as personal shopping and dog walking to many of the Internet-based businesses such as selling items on eBay, iOffer, eBid, Etsy, Shopify, Bonanza, Craiglist, Rakuten, Walmart marketplace, Amazon marketplace and other auction sites for others.

Simply improve on an existing product or service. You could simply look out for products or services you have a passion for to improve their quality, value, effectiveness, efficiency, reliability, and much more.

Launch an accidental business. Create something that you'll love working on even if it never takes off. Which, rather perversely, is also the best way to make sure it's something cool enough and passion-filled enough to be loved by other people. Build a community around it. Then, finally, try to figure out how to make some cash from it.

Look ahead. What do you believe consumers will want or be looking out for in three to six months from now, a year from now, that they can't find today on the market? Future trends are a big thing these days. Henry Ford (Ford Motors), Sir Tim Berners-Lee (World Wide Web), Bill Gates (Microsoft PC), Steve Jobs (Apple), Mark Zuckerberg (Facebook), Larry Page and Sergey Brin (Google), Elon Musk (Tesla and SpaceX), Jack Dorsey, Noah Glass, Biz Stone and Evan Williams (Twitter), Travis Kalanick and Garret Camp (Uber), Jan Koum and Brian Acton (WhatsApp), Jeff Bezos (Amazon), Jack Ma (Alibaba), Oprah Winfrey (OWN), Sir Richard Branson (Virgin), Brian Chesky, Joe Gebbia and Nathan Blecharczyk (Airbnb), and many others have and still look to project the needs of consumers ahead of time.

Fund other people's ideas. You may be someone who has resources but no time to get involved in the day-to-day running of business. You could make available your cash to others to turn ideas into viable businesses, and share in the profits. There are so many people at both ends. There are those with great ideas but with no resources. And there are those with plenty of cash sitting in bank accounts earning next to nothing, by way of interest, with the banks investing it for their own gain and charging all sorts of fees on the money.

Invest in stocks. There are various opportunities in trading in stocks both for short-term and long-term gains. These include spread betting, forex trading and derivatives to simple buying and selling of shares. Always seek expert advice first as you also indulge in your own common-sense research on the right stocks and price.

Write for cash. How about writing for cash? You can contribute to various established blogging sites and get paid. Or you could create a blog of your own, write interesting stuff, build a great following, and with Google Adsense, you could be on your way into making some good money. Start by searching online for some of these sites:
- www.ezinearticles.com,
- www.hubpages.com, and
- www.blogger.com.

The list above is not definitive. It should be a starting point as you think about the opportunities available to you. Many moneymaking ideas are yet to be explored, and with the Internet you have an almost entire globe you can potentially sell to.

Some very interesting websites to look at for some very great inspiring ideas and trends include
- www.entrepreneur.com,
- www.rightbiz.co.uk,
- www.businessopportunitiesandideas.com, and
- www.trendwatching.com.

Having gone through the above and potentially got an idea or two, ask yourself, "Do I know about anything that anyone wants – but they either cannot get it or they have to go through too much hassle to get it?" It could be a product, service, or both. If you do, then that is a great place to start. While you do that, consider whether you can:

- Create or come up with something people want and charge money for it.
- Produce something other people wish they had. If you can do that and you can reach people who will buy your product then you could have the beginnings of a business.

- Channel your energy into doing something you are good at, and provide a useful service to people you know will pay for it.

Let's hear what some well-known entrepreneurs have to say about this:

Thomas Edison once said, "*I never perfected an invention that I did not think about in terms of the service it might give others… I find out what the world needs, then I proceed to invent.*" I couldn't agree more with the great inventor.

Richard Branson, founder of Virgin Group, on the other hand, said, "*Business opportunities are like buses, there's always another one coming.*"[43] To this I ask the question, are you ready to jump on board?

Madam C.J. Walker, America's first black female millionaire (creator of a popular line of African-American hair care products), said, "*I had to make my own living and my own opportunity! But I made it! Don't sit down and wait for the opportunities to come. Get up and make them!*"[44] I guess in other words, if there are no opportunities, it's time for you to create your own.

Interestingly, most organic start-up ideas usually don't seem like start-up ideas at first. That's because a lot of ideas seem like just another quick and dirty solution to a problem. It is best to focus on developing the idea and worry less about the stigma attached to being a new business start-up. Building a business is a foundation for creating value and meaning.

With all the positives and opportunities that come with using social media as a platform for doing business, it has in a way become a limiting factor in some instances. When it comes to identifying opportunities, many people narrow the hunt, looking only at what can be done via social networks or tech related businesses.

I absolutely believe in the great potential of social media, and believe that not being a part of it is just not an option in this business age. Being smart about social media allows you to develop and maintain your own network of potential customers, partners and clients. However, none of this matters unless you have a good idea and you set out to do something about it.

In the current economic climate where many cannot find needed security in their 9-5 jobs, I believe there is no better time than now for you to take action. Even if it's only on a part-time basis as you TRY it out. As Nolan Bushnell, founder of Atari and Chuck E. Cheese's, wisely put it: *"The critical ingredient is getting off your butt and doing something. It's as simple as that. A lot of people have ideas, but there are few who decide to do something about them now. Not tomorrow. Not next week. But today. The true entrepreneur is a doer, not a dreamer."*[45]

Also, never forget that every big business starts as a small business.

I sincerely hope by the time you finish this book, you will be among those who stumbled across the opportunities and got up to take advantage of them.

6

A FEW BUSINESS IDEAS WORTH CHECKING OUT

In this chapter I am going to point out a few areas with some specific ideas for your consideration from anywhere in the world. I like to believe that from the previous chapter you were able to identify some potential opportunities worth researching.

If not, this chapter will give you another chance to explore some specific ideas.

> **Agribusiness** – According to the World Bank, food agribusiness is a $5 trillion industry that represents 10% of global consumer spending. Significant opportunities exist all along the agribusiness value chain in both developed and developing economies. This includes businesses to connect producers, farmers, and entrepreneurs to domestic, regional and global markets, directly or indirectly to other agribusinesses

in the chain. Other opportunities include storage facilities, processing to add value and reduce wastage, marketing, distribution, etc.

Consulting on sectors you are an expert in, tapping into your experience to help others. The global consultancy industry has seen year-on-year growth over the past 5 decades and it is currently estimated to be worth $250 billion.

Content creation – According to analysts from Technavio, the content marketing industry, for instance, is projected to be worth $412.88 billion by 2021.

Copy writing – slogans, taglines, company offerings, website copy, brochure and pitches

Creative services – As more entrepreneurs become brand conscious, many are upgrading to give their business a professional make-over with sleek and glossy visuals to help them stand out.

Design and create online academic courses for primary, high school, college, and university students. With the increasing penetration of Internet access worldwide, the global online education market is projected to reach $319.167 billion in 2025 from $187.877 billion in 2019.

Digital marketing – this goes way beyond social media management

Fitness, health and wellness experts – The global wellness economy is set to exceed $4.5 trillion, and as the world becomes more health conscious, creators of wellness products and service providers are in demand.

Interior design – According to a Global Interior Design Industry report[46] published at the end of 2019, the interior design market is projected to grow by $109.3 billion, driven by a compounded growth of 8.7%.

Language courses and tutors as people seek to learn new languages to make themselves versatile and able to function anywhere.

Mobile app development – Mobile applications have become part of our everyday lives. The market value of this industry is currently projected to reach $407.31 billion by 2026 from $106.27 billion in 2018.

Online business courses – E-learning is set to reach $325bn by 2025. The most searched courses in 2019 were Python Scripting, Online Marketing, Project Management, Excel, and Time Management.

Agribusiness in Africa – farming and agribusiness value chain - wholesalers, retailers, processors or manufacturers, exporters, etc.

Fintech – Mobile payment options continue to gather speed as more and more people want to do away with cash post COVID-19.

Digital education – Traditional classroom teaching is increasingly being challenged, more so in the pandemic season and potentially beyond. Online educational platforms have become and will continue to be dominant in the near future.

Digital health – Technology can help bridge healthcare gaps by providing software for self-assessment and symptom checking. Travel restrictions during COVID-19 have highlighted the need for more nations to reconsider the development of its own high-quality healthcare infrastructure. This throws up many new opportunities in Africa and the rest of the developing world.

Food delivery services – Examples of some of the existing companies in this space include: Blue Apron, Hello fresh, Home Chef, Freshly, Gobble, Uber Eats, GrubHub, DoorDash and many more springing up. You could focus on a niche segment of this market.

Services industry – contactless systems, enhanced delivery services, remote banking services

Gaming Industry – new ways of disseminating content and promoting small businesses, online cooking classes, and virtual tours with visits to landmarks, etc.

Healthcare and health technology – pharmaceuticals, supplements, medical devices, personal protective equipment (PPE) (a company in UK producing hand sanitiser is now worth £30m), telemedicine, smart hospitals and online consultations, digital medical assistants, apps and mini-apps, self-diagnosing medical devices

Electrical appliances – dishwashers and washing machines, sterilisation machines (with personnel to offer that service worldwide), sweeping robots

Wellness and wellbeing in the workplace – reconfiguration of workspaces in the wake of new social distancing rules and beyond. Working from home tools and things to enhance the experience.

Online streaming – Netflix, Hulu, Qibi, Disney Plus, Amazon Prime, and smaller ones that have gradually emerged to gain new clients and patronage. Producers and makers are releasing new movies online.

Animation creators are benefitting the most.[47] Nigerian producers are selling lots of content to global online streaming giants.

Accounting services

Affordable luxury items

Auto repair services

Baby and post-pregnancy products and services

Bookkeeping

Bulk food sales

Cooking classes

Creating digital entertainment for kids

Currency trading

Day care services

Debt collection agencies

Electronic gadget repairs

Food trucks

Home food delivery

Home staging

IT technical support

Mobile hair and beauty experts

Repair services professional

Resume-writing services

Social media management

Virtual assistant

In conclusion, I like what Brian Chesky, Co-founder of Airbnb said, *"If we tried to think of a good idea, we wouldn't have been able to think of a good idea. You just have to find the solution for a problem in your own life."*[48] And whatever you do, *"Be creative while inventing ideas, but be disciplined while implementing them."*[49] – Amit Kalantri. Because it takes more than just identifying opportunities and coming up with ideas; you need the discipline, dedication and commitment to start and engage with the process to realise your goals.

7

STEPS IN DEVELOPING AN IDEA

> *"If you have ideas, you have the main asset you need, and there isn't any limit to what you can do with your business and your life. Ideas are any man's greatest assets."*
> Harvey S. Firestone, *an American businessman and founder of Firestone Tire and Rubber Company*

A good new idea is often the basis for starting a business. In the previous chapter, we established that you could spot a gap in the market and start a business that provides a product or service to fill it, or come up with ways to improve an existing product.

Identifying an opportunity or spotting an idea is a great start. However, developing the idea into a viable product or service is a critical part of the process. Unfortunately, there are those who become so consumed by their passionate desire to start a business that it clouds their judgment in making an informed decision. It is not enough to fall in love with an idea and pursue it. Rather, it is necessary to assess how viable this business idea is. A business must be able to grow and be – or become – profitable over time, and must also be able to transform itself, adapting to changing times and customer needs over its lifetime or for the foreseeable future.

Asking yourself few simple questions can make all the difference between succeeding and failing. For a business to be viable, it must have positive answers to the following basic questions:

- Does my business idea meet a specific need?
- Is it an answer to a specific question?
- Is it a solution to a specific problem?
- Can I offer something different from what may already be in existence?
- Is what I want to offer going out of fashion, trend, or being taken over by new technology?
- Is it a regulated business, and can I meet the requirements in a cost-effective way?
- Can I produce the item or provide the service at a reasonable cost?
- Can I put a price on my products or services?
- Are people willing to pay for it?

- Can I make a profit at a price people are willing to pay for my products or services?

Understanding the market and the needs of customers, and tailoring your products and services to meet these needs is a great way forward.

With the subject of viability in mind, it is important to identify which business you want to start. You may start as a retail business, a wholesale business, a manufacturing business, or a service provider.

You will also need to define the subject of the business. That is, what you will sell. The final question to answer should be how you will sell the product or service.

Let us consider a few steps that can help us turn an idea into a fully-fledged viable business.

Try to learn something new every day. Having conceived an idea or two, it may be necessary to talk to other businesspeople, such as a business coach or consultant, business owners or entrepreneurs, friends, or neighbours – anyone who looks interesting and will talk to you about what you are considering and give feedback on what they think. However, exercise a lot of discretion in knowing who to talk to. In the words of Thomas Berger, "*The art and science of asking questions is the source of all knowledge.*"[50] Browse the web, and read magazines, books, and biographies of entrepreneurs, expanding your knowledge each day. You will be surprised what you will find. You may even end up discovering something completely new to pursue other than your original idea.

Keep a written record of your ideas. Whenever you are inspired by an idea, write it down. There is no limit to the number of ideas you can write down. You are more likely to remember them and can always refer to them should you forget. Writing down any idea that comes to mind can help you differentiate between ideas. It's very important to be as specific as possible at this stage. For instance, an idea such as "A Clothing or Book Store" is different from "An Online Clothing or Book Store." For instance, one idea could bring you the quickest return on your investment, another require the least amount of capital, and a third require less commitment to get it off the ground and make your idea a reality.

Draw a mind map. Often, to have a pictorial view of how your idea is coming together, drawing a mind map is a very good way to go. A mind map is simply a diagram used to represent words and ideas, linked to and arranged around a central key word or idea. It helps to generate, visualise, structure, and classify ideas. It also acts as an aid in study, organisation, problem solving, decision making, and writing. Check out some mind mapping tools – www.mural.co, www.mindmeister.com, other apps include Scapple, Ayoa, Milanote, Miro and many more.

Research other conditions out there. Evaluate potential competition, keeping notes on what you find. A thorough assessment and market research at this stage will help you establish whether there is a market for your product or service. Some of the questions you want your brief market research to answer should be:

- Is this product or service going to satisfy a market need?
- Who are my potential customers, and where can they be found?
- What competition is out there? Is it direct or indirect, local, national, or international?
- How distinct is my product from what is being offered by the competition?
- Can the product stand the test of changing trends, or take advantage of it before it dies out?
- Does the law of the land allow for such a business to be established?
- At what prices are consumers prepared to buy my product, and can I make any profit at any stage?

Synthesise ideas. Put two or more unrelated ideas together and brainstorm it. For instance, setting up a bookstore to providing a courier service or selling clothes online to offering a professional secretarial or accountancy service, or manufacturing a new brand of fruit juice to importing rice, etc. That helps to make a firm decision on the way forward.

Sleep on the idea. Go away for a while, thinking of something else. Often your subconscious mind will continue to work on the problem and will come up with new ideas or refinements to the original idea.

Talk about your ideas. Talk especially with those close to you and who have your best interests at heart. Brainstorm your idea with friends, colleagues, or staff. They can give different perspectives on the idea and may know if there is anyone else doing the same thing out there. In the words of Robert Quillen, *"Discussion is an exchange of knowledge."*[51] Or simply write down how you would have explained your idea to another person. This helps you spot flaws or areas for improvement. Ultimately though, *"don't let others convince you that the idea is good when your guts tells you it's bad."*[52] – Kevin Rose, co-founder of Digg.

Consider the impact of new technologies. Given the pace of technological advancement, you may need to think about whether your idea can take advantage of an opportunity created by any new technology available or yet to be developed. An example is online trading as opposed to the more traditional way of trading from a fixed location. Many businesses are moving online and employing tools that enable them to cut costs, improve efficiency and open themselves up to a wider audience beyond their locality.

Consider the impact of social trends. It is also very important to consider whether social trends may affect the design or demand for your product or service. Examples are concerns about global warming and carbon footprints, or increasing demand for organic food.

Write your business plan. Inasmuch as I will not insist on you writing a business plan before you start, it makes a huge difference if you invest in one beforehand. *"If you don't know where you are going, you'll end up someplace else."*[53] – Yogi Berra. I have provided a comprehensive guide in this book to help you realistically assess the viability and potential success of your idea and chosen business model and processes.

Protect your idea. You should confine and protect your idea. Keep your idea as private as possible except, of course, with the trusted and respected individuals who are part of the process of development. It will be smart to stop talking about your idea once you have finalised the specific one to pursue, until such time as it's ready for the market, and any licensing necessary to protect the idea has been secured. It takes wisdom to know when to speak and when to shut up.

Whatever idea you decide on, understand how you think your intended business will work. Identify who your customers are going to be, what problem you are going to solve, how your product or service is going to meet consumers' needs, how your customers will find your product, who will sell it, who will deliver it, etc. You must have clearly stated objectives and understand how you intend to achieve them and succeed.

I hope this process has helped you fine-tune your identified opportunity. In the next chapter, we will highlight a few factors that, when taken into consideration, can help put you on "top of the game" as you enter the market.

8

CREATING A DISTINCTION FOR YOUR PRODUCT OR SERVICE

> *"You're just anybody without your identity."*
> Grenville Main, *MD of DNA Design*

Having gone through the basic steps of fine-tuning your idea, let us look at how you are going to distinguish yourself from the existing market.

What is your Unique Selling Point (USP)?

In the words of Tom Chappell, an American businessman and manufacturer, *"Success means never letting the competition define you. Instead you have to define yourself based on a point of view you care deeply about."*[54]

To be able to take your share of the existing market, you will need to find a way to make consumers want what you are offering, outside of what already exists. Establishing your USP is very important. It should focus on how your product or service will benefit the customer and what makes you totally stand out from the competition. This can be summed up in just a few words that becomes something like the catchphrase of your advertising jingle. It may also be expressed as a summary of what you do and how you do it better or differently to others. Do everything possible not to be tempted to choose a phrase that becomes counterproductive because you cannot fulfil the promise. Your USP also helps protect your idea in the marketplace. You can establish your uniqueness by:

- Understanding the core needs of your customers and market.
- Taking the time to discover any untapped area in your market and exploiting it.
- Taking advantage of technology and the Internet with its unlimited scope and potential.
- Taking advantage of established systems and building on them without needing to start from scratch. With a bit of adjustment, a big difference can be made to an existing business model.

Or simply ask yourself questions such as:

- What are you going to do? What is your speciality or niche area going to be?
- Who are your customers? Look at the demographics: age, gender, interests, location, national or international markets, etc.
- What do these customers want? Is it a kind of flexible service, low prices, availability of your product or service locally, a trusted source, or something else that will attract customers to your business?
- How are you going to do it? Will there be something special, unusual, or significant about the way you will do business? Fast turnaround, free delivery, personal service, etc?

Developing Your Brand Right From The Start

> "A brand is not saying what it is, it's what the customer THINKS it is."[55]
> Karen Katz, CEO of Neiman Marcus

Closely associated with USP is branding. Unfortunately, most people start their businesses with none of that in mind. Often when I ask clients about their brand, initial reactions tend to be to shrug it off. Some make statements like, "What has that got to do with my small business?" Let's face it, Nike, Microsoft, Apple, KFC, McDonalds, Coca-Cola, Toyota, Ford, Mercedes, Walmart, Tesco, BP, Shell, and the many other established brands out there started as small backyard, tabletop, and garage businesses. You could be excused for overlooking it in the past, but not in the 21st Century where globalisation offers so many options to clients and businesses all around us. I strongly encourage you to have the development of your brand at the back of your mind right from the start of your business.

Let's establish what branding really means. A brand is basically a name used to identify and distinguish a specific product, service, or business. It can also be defined as the image of the product in the market. The **American Marketing Association** defines a brand as *"a name, term, design, symbol or any other feature that identifies one seller's good or service as distinct from those of other sellers."*

Branding is, therefore, about getting your prospects to see you as the only one who provides a solution to their problem, and not just about getting your target market to choose you over the competition. Brand strategist Kerry Light once said, *"The primary focus of your brand message must be on how special you are, not how cheap you are. The goal must be to sell the distinctive quality of the brand."*[56]

Building a brand is like building a city. As a city has a network of components such as roads, houses, libraries, and shopping centres, so does a brand. Each of the components has its own unique network but still has to fit into the ultimate plan to make the city complete. A city is planned and not built in a day. It's built one component, one day at a time. So is a brand.

A good brand, among other things must:

- Clarify your position in the business.
- Clearly deliver your message.
- Motivate your buyers and deliver on your brand promise.
- Consistently reinforce your identity.
- Confirm your credibility.
- Connect to your target potential emotionally.
- Create loyalty and enthusiasm among your consumers.

An established brand, over time, brings with it a host of benefits such as:

- Adding value to your business.
- Developing a loyalty base that cuts cost on marketing and advertising.

- Increasing your turnover.
- Projecting an image of quality in your business.
- Projecting an image of a large and established business that has been around long enough to be well known.
- Allowing you to link together several different products in your business. As you put your brand name on every product and service you sell, customers for one product will be more likely to buy one of your other products.

The question I guess you must be asking now is, "What are the specific things I will need to focus on at this stage to ensure I start on the right footing?"

A memorable and easy-to-remember name – A good brand name should be easy to pronounce, attract attention, be easy to remember, be easy to recognise, suggest product benefits and usage, suggest the company or product image, be attractive, stand out among a group of other brands, distinguish the product's positioning in relation to the competition, and be protectable under trademark law. Of course, if you have your eyes on the international market (which is what I encourage every new business to aim at by taking advantage of the enormous platform handed to us by globalisation and the Internet), then you ought to be mindful of the meaning of your chosen name in other languages. Lexicon states, *"A brand name is more than a word. It is the beginning of a* *conversation."* You can check on the meaning of names in other languages at www.babelfish.com. With the level of customer awareness and sensitivities in this decade the last thing you want to do is alienate a section of society because you failed to check what your desired name meant to others.

A professionally designed distinctive logo – Symbols and images are much more noticeable than text. Diane Ackerman stated, *"The visual image is a kind of tripwire for the emotions."*[57] The image size, quality, and colours deserve important consideration. Thankfully, there are so many logo design apps to help you create one. Some of the most popular platforms include: www.wix.com, www.tailorbrands.com, www.canva.com, www.looka.com, Logo Maker, Logoscopic, Logopit Plus, and many such apps and platforms. Having said that, on platforms such as www.upwork.com and www.fiverr.com you can get a professional to do one for you on a budget.

A catchy phrase or slogan

Professionally designed stationary – This includes business cards, letterhead, websites, and brochures. However, it's in using them that you get people associating with it.

Strategic advertising – Use online, local and national newspapers, magazine, radio, television, directories, outdoor and transit, direct mail catalogues and leaflets, web-based ads such as Google Ads, public relations, and word of mouth.

As a new business, there might not be enough money to embark on all these right from the start. However, the purpose at this stage is to have all these factors in mind so that if you can only afford the logo, you do not just do anything just for the sake of it. There are a lot of free business card design platforms and offers on the Internet. However, the quality of the materials and processing are mostly below standard. A little search-and-spend will get you a professionally designed quality logo, business card, and letterhead, often offered as a complete package, which communicates value and seriousness to potential businesses and clients. Also understand that *"a brand is a living entity – and it is enriched or undermined cumulatively over time, the product of a thousand small gestures."*[58] –Michael Eisner, Former Chairman and CEO of Disney.

There are so many aspects of branding that we can talk about under brand management. However, at this stage all I want you to consider are the benefits and how to develop your brand as you work your way through the start-up stages.

In conclusion, do all you must to be distinctive and keep repeating your message. Be consistent, be persistent, evolve with the times as much as is necessary, stand for something, be linked with something specific in the minds of your consumers, and protect your distinctiveness.

To protect your brand, it must be properly trademarked, ensuring that other people cannot use your brand for their gain. You can trademark words, names, logos, or designs or a combination of these. A trademark will give a business an exclusive right to use the trademark and may lawfully prosecute any parties that use the same trademark in the future. For a business name to be trademarked in most jurisdictions or countries it may have to be established through actual use in the marketplace, or through registration of the mark with the trademarks office or trademarks registry in that country or jurisdiction. However, in some jurisdictions, trademark rights may be established through either or both means. Please note, registering a company name with the body responsible for registering a business in most countries, be it Companies House in the UK, Federal States Business Entity Registration Offices in the USA, Registrar of Companies in (ROC) in India, Registrar of Companies – also known as Companies and Intellectual Property Commission (CIPC) – in South Africa, Registrar General Department in Ghana, The Corporate Affairs Commission (CAC) of Nigeria, Liberia Business Registry in Monrovia, etc., does not necessarily mean that you have a trademark of your company name even though no other business can be registered as your name.

9

PROVEN STRATEGIES FOR GROWTH

> "Change is not a destination, just as hope is not a strategy."
> Rudy Giuliani, an American Attorney and former Mayor of New York City

> "Sound strategy starts with having the right goal… Strategy is about making choices, trade-offs; it's about deliberately choosing to be different… The company without a strategy is willing to try anything."
> Michael Porter, Professor at Harvard Business School, and a leading authority on company strategy and the competitiveness of nations and regions

A business strategy clearly helps you articulate the direction a business will pursue and the steps it will take to achieve these goals. A good strategy should clearly differentiate a business from its competitors. Adopting or crafting a better strategy helps a business establish a clear framework for subsequent decisions, giving it an edge in the marketplace right from the start. Your understanding of these strategies will help you choose the winning approach to success.

In this chapter, we will discuss marketing, pricing, advertising, and sales as core strategies that need serious consideration for you to succeed in business. However, the growth and increasing role of social media as an important marketing tool cannot be ... ignored. I will briefly discuss a few important facts you need to know in taking advantage of this.

Marketing Strategy

Marketing is essentially about getting the right product or service in front of the people who will want to buy it. A marketing strategy helps you identify and communicate what your business offers to your target market, whereas a marketing plan helps you implement your marketing strategy. A good marketing strategy should help you address the specific needs of the different customer groups. Contents of the marketing strategy should be measurable and actionable and work to differentiate your company and products from the competition. The objectives of your marketing strategy should also establish specific goals, such as, "Our goal is to capture 10% of the existing market in the next twelve months and 25% by the end of three years in ten cities," or, "We want to achieve a turnover of £1 million in the next two years within the southwest region." It must also take into account how your business strengths and weaknesses will affect your marketing.

A workable strategy should help you:

- Identify the specific customer segments you are targeting and your positioning in that market segment
- Identify how to serve your targeted customer segment or group, i.e. define the benefits they are looking for and how you intend to meet that, and the technology you intend to use
- Establish your marketing objectives, such as your intended market share, growth, how you intend to enter the market, and how you intend to increase awareness of what you are offering
- Work out what mix of marketing tools such as products, price, place, and promotion you will use to help you deliver the needed benefits to your customers and beat the competition.

Answering the following questions can help you create a good basis for putting a workable strategy together:

- How do you define what your company is?
- What are the products or services your company will provide?
- Who are your target customers?
- Which marketing category will you establish yourself in?
- Does your company intend to become a market category leader, challenger, follower, or niche player?
- What are the unique characteristics of your products or services that distinguish you from the competition?
- What are your pricing policies? Will your price be above, below, or at parity with your competitors, and are you going to lead, follow, or ignore changes in competitors' pricing?
- Through which distribution channels will your products or services be made available to the target market?
- How will your advertising and promotions convey the unique characteristics of your product or service?
- Which research and development activities or market research plans are unique to your business?

- How can you describe the image or personality of your company and its products or services?

One of the most commonly used marketing strategies by new and small businesses is the growth strategy. The focus of this strategy is to simply help you identify the way you will use products and markets or customers to achieve a desired level of growth in your business. Here are some growth strategies:

Current product for current market. This strategy is used to increase your share of an existing market. It is usually implemented by finding new customers or raising customers' awareness of your current products and services.

Current product for new market. This is a strategy of finding and entering new markets with your current product or service. This new market could be a new segment of the market, a new country, or a new region.

New product for current market. This approach simply demands you improve your existing products and services or develop new ones to enhance the benefits you deliver to your customers.

New product for new market. This strategy involves adopting new ways of doing business, which could carry higher risk and cost. It's more than simply offering new products or services in a new market. There is a bit more risk involved in adopting this strategy because you are more or less charting uncharted territory, with totally new products for an entirely new market.

Your marketing strategy can only benefit your business if you use it. It is also important to ensure that you have the operational capacity and processes to fulfil any extra orders, ensure timely delivery, and provide any extra services efficiently and reliably in handling the extra business your strategy generates.

Pricing Strategy

Pricing strategies are sometimes not given much consideration by new businesses. However, they are a major determining factor in the survival or success of a business and a workable component of a good marketing strategy. Understanding this strategy and getting it right will positively affect your revenues and profit. For some businesses, it's simply looking at what is being charged by competitors and setting prices accordingly. A lower or higher price can significantly change both sales volumes and gross margins and, subsequently, profits.

Understanding some of the factors that influence how much people are willing to pay for goods and services will be very helpful at this stage. People generally pay based on the:

- Price of substitute products or services in the marketplace.
- Price of related products or services available.
- Cost of the problem a product or service solves.
- The status associated with using or owning such a product or service.
- Cost of a problem the product or service prevents.
- Location where the product or service is provided.
- Persons using the product or service.
- Revenues that can be generated from owning the product or service.
- Customer service and support provided both before and after the service or product is sold.
- Guaranteed warranty period.

Establishing your pricing objectives is undoubtedly among the most basic and important things to do. However, you can only accomplish the stated objectives after taking the following factors into consideration.

Cost of production – It is critical to take into account both the variable and fixed cost components of producing a product or providing a service. Variable cost is the cost that changes according to the change in the volume of production. Fixed cost, on the other hand, does not change unless there is a major expansion of the business. A pricing policy should cover both types of cost for the business to turn a profit.

Position in the market – It is important to determine whether pricing is going to be a key factor in positioning yourself in the market. Positioning your price as an exclusive luxury product, for instance, demands a different approach than operating as a discount store. Whereas the discount store has to keep its prices as low as possible consistent with its objectives, pricing an exclusive luxury product too low may hurt the product's image. Pricing should, therefore, be consistent with the positioning of the product in the market. The idea of "you get what you pay for" subconsciously has some level of influence on how the price of a product is perceived.

Demand of the product or service – Good basic market research should help you determine how your price will affect the demand of your product. Asking potential customers how much they will be willing to pay can help you decide the price that can give you the right balance of turnover. A simple questionnaire asking how much respondents are willing to pay for a service or product can help, especially in the case of small, new start-ups. A larger firm or one with more resources may be able to hire a market research company.

Environmental factors – It is equally important to find out what external factors may affect your pricing strategy. Consider the implication of your pricing on your competitors. To set a price too low may be inviting an unpleasant risk of price wars. On the other hand, setting a price too high may attract a large number of competitors who want to share in the profits. Legally, a firm might not have total freedom in setting its price at any level. For instance, pricing too low may be considered predatory pricing, offering different prices for different consumers might be seen as price discrimination, or colluding with competitors to price a product or service may be illegal, which it is in most economies.

The above factors should help you establish what your pricing objectives must be. The objectives could be:

- Seeking to maximise profit in the short term. This is not a very good objective if it results in lower long-term profits.
- Seeking to maximise current revenue with little regard for profit margins. This enables a business to increase its market share and lower cost to ensure long-term profitability.

- Reducing long-term costs by maximising the number of units sold or the number of customers served to increase profit in the long run.
- Maximising profit margins on each unit sold. This is used particularly for items or products that are sold in small quantities, such as handmade automobiles and artwork.
- Using the price to signal high quality or a high level of service in an attempt to position the product as the quality leader. At the other extreme is to be the low-cost leader as a way of differentiating yourself from the competition.
- Surviving by covering just the cost. This is used especially when the market is in decline or over capacity.
- Seeking price stabilisation just to avoid price wars and maintain a moderate and stable profit margin. Many new businesses do this.

With the understanding gained from the objectives and factors that should be considered when determining the price of a product, let us now look at some pricing methods you may adopt. However, it is important to establish that there is no one right way to price a product or service.

> ***Cost-plus pricing*** *–* This is among the most common methods. The price is set at total cost of production plus a certain profit margin. Always remember that

the cost of production includes both fixed cost and variable cost at the current volume.

Target return pricing – This means setting a price to achieve a return on investment. You want to recoup your investment within a certain time frame by pricing your product to achieve that set investment target.

Value-based pricing – With this method, you set the price based on the value of the product or service to the customer. This is used especially when the product or service significantly saves more for the customer.

Psychological pricing – The price is set based on factors such as what a consumer perceives to be fair, popular price points (the price at which people are much more willing to buy a certain type of product) and signals of product quality (are you a low-cost leader or high quality product or service provider?).

Finally, let me tie all the above together and give you a shot at some of the best strategies:

Cost plus mark-up – With this strategy, you decide the profit you want to make and add it to your cost to determine your selling price.

Competitive pricing – This is the opposite of cost plus mark-up. With this strategy, you use your competitors' prices as benchmarks to price your products or service. You could decide to price your products slightly above, below, or as your competitors, depending on your positioning strategy.

Trade discounting – This strategy seeks to attract business from profitable customer categories (i.e. customer segments who contribute most of your profits) offering those special discounts, either as lower prices on certain products or free product rewards.

Loss leader – This involves selling below cost in order to attract more customers with the belief that they will buy other high-profit items. This is one strategy commonly used by most supermarkets.

Bundling and quantity discounts – This is where customers are rewarded for larger purchases through bundling or quantity discounts. It is done by setting the per-unit price lower should a customer purchase more instead of one or charging less when a customer buys several related items in a single shopping trip.

Versioning – This is where you sell a general product in different configurations, so the basic version is either offered free or at a very low price and the other services are available at a higher price.

Close out – This is best used when there is excess inventory to get rid of. The goal here is to minimise losses instead of making profits. Stocks are sold at steep discounts to reduce or avoid storage costs.

Good pricing requires good market research. Find people who will be potential customers of your products, understand their needs and provide what will meet their needs. Settle that, and determine your price based on your pricing objectives and existing or applicable factors to ensure the growth and profitability of your business. It is equally important to focus on adding value to your products as much as possible instead of relying solely on pricing to make your product much more competitive.

Advertising Strategy

> *"Nothing except the mint can make money without advertising."*
> Thomas B. Macaulay

Every business needs to promote itself constantly to reach out to its customers and potential customers. Advertising is basically the methods used by a business to publicise and position its products and services to its target market. This includes the use of salespeople, product launches, brand name and image, promotion of the product in retail and wholesale outlets, press releases and other public relations activities, and special offers.

An advertising strategy must support your marketing strategy. The aim is to attract the customer, capture his or her attention, and leave an impression of interest and some level of curiosity.

> "Good advertising does not just circulate information. It penetrates the public mind with desires and belief."[59]
> Leo Burnett.

It may be the way customers form their first impressions of your business. You must use different ways of thinking and creative strategies to create slogans, sounds, and impressions that will communicate the information you want to send to your intended audience.

> "Advertising says to people, 'Here's what we've got. Here's what it will do for you. Here's how to get it'."
> Leo Burnett

Just stop with me for a moment and consider this. As we embark on our daily routines, we see or hear of something being advertised. It gets our attention and, if it's of relevance to us, we get interested. If it has a resemblance to what we need or have been thinking about, what do we do? We desire it and even plan how we will own and use it.

A good advertisement should, therefore:

- Generate awareness of your business.
- Provide basic information on your business contact details.
- Result in increased sales by letting your potential customers know about your product or services.
- Inform customers about latest offers, new product launches, and improvements to your services and products.
- Make you stand out, creating a distinctive brand for your business and establishing you as the first choice for customers.
- Enable you to develop a unique position and niche in the market.
- Be attractive enough to cause suppliers to want to do business with you and even entice potential employees.

A well-planned advertisement will have long-range benefits for any small or new business. Let's look at some of the methods or mediums by which you can advertise your business.

Word of mouth – Spread the word among relatives, friends, colleagues, and former colleagues who will tell others, and others will tell others, and on and on.

Your voicemail – As interesting as it may sound, changing the message on your voicemail to reflect the fact that you are now in business for yourself is a simple great start.

Business cards – Have them professionally designed with a touch of excellence and quality. Never be without them and hand them out at every opportunity.

Flyers – There are many places (local groceries, libraries, cafes, etc.) that will allow you to display your flyers freely. Note however that increasingly, electronic flyers are more in use and are shared across various social media and messaging platforms much more effectively.

Website – Create a website, which is almost free to do these days. Alternatively, you can get professionals to do it for you at very little cost. Advertise your site to the world on the Internet via Google Ads and many other platforms offering pay-per-click. A website helps you centralise all your business and gives you somewhere to send people to buy from you. Place your web address in your e-mail signature.

Signs and stickers – Bumper stickers and magnetic signs on your car is another way to go.

Clothes – Wear your ads by putting them on your t-shirts, sweatshirts, baseball caps, pens, etc.

Direct mailing – Place your business cards and flyers in your outgoing mail.

Free classifieds – There are a lot of free classifieds websites on the Internet that will help you place your advertisements for free.

Send promotions with invoices – Sending promotional materials with invoices, asking recipients to "refer a friend" is a great way forward.

Yellow pages – A lot of people also rely on the Yellow Pages to find businesses.

Newspapers – Local and national newspapers often offer special ad features for new and small businesses to advertise their products and services.

Magazines – Choose a magazine that your target market subscribes to and place an ad.

Professional and business groups – A lot of such bodies have exclusive advertising opportunities for its members, from free listing on their websites to inclusion in their directories.

Radio – Advertising on a local radio station is another approach that must be taken advantage of as it tends to be effective and much less expensive than TV and even some newspapers.

Bus stop bench – Advertising on benches in public areas and active bus stops is another way of advertising.

Vehicles – Ads can be placed on your vehicle; from custom graphics to magnetic signs on top of vehicles to removable magnetic signs that can be taken off anytime you want.

Trade show participation – Trade shows put together by local business associations and other similar organisations are usually much cheaper to take advantage of than nationally organised commercial and international shows. Of course, your target audience matters when determining the shows worth signing up to.

Email – Mailing lists generated by your business via surveys, customer feedback, etc., can be used to advertise your products or services.

Community involvement – Getting involved in your locality either as a business or citizen is a very effective way of making yourself known to potential customers.

Join other businesses – Combining resources with other businesses can greatly work to your advantage. You can do so with complementing businesses.

Local council website – Advertise on websites that provide business information for your local areas. Many local councils and municipalities have local business listing pages on their sites for small businesses.

Local and national TV ads – Small and local TV stations have promotional offers for small businesses, from documentaries to being featured on business news, all within the budget of small businesses.

You are most likely not going to be effective by using *all* the above methods. Your best shot will be to assess your advertising needs and choose the best option (some of which are almost **free**) with your objectives and budget in mind. I will however advice strongly against using just free options or platforms, because they often come with limitations. For most platforms just a little spend gives your ad better and more strategic exposure.

Here are ten principles that can guide you in getting the best of effective advertising:

1. Use one message that is simple, catchy, short, easy to remember, and consistent. It must personally communicate to the individual reader. In the words of William Bernbach, a former advertising director, *"Advertising doesn't create a product advantage. It can only convey it."*[60]

2. Give your ad a relevant headline other than the name of your business. *"If your advertising goes unnoticed, everything else is academic."* – William Bernbach

3. For effectiveness, focus and create unique ad messages for each specific audience or target group.

4. The message must communicate the benefits of what you are offering. Ensure your advertisement avoids bold claims that your product or service cannot deliver. *"Telling lies does not work in advertising."* – Stanisław Lec[61]

5. Create an ad that generates curiosity for customers to want to know more, even more than selling a product or service. In the words of Peter

Nivio Zarlenga, *"In our factory, we make lipstick. In our advertising, we sell hope."*[62]

6. All ads must have your contact details, such as telephone number, social media handles, e-mail addresses, websites, and company address, displayed very visibly.

7. Do not advertise via any medium just because your competitors are advertising in that medium. Choose platforms strategically in relation to your target audience.

8. Your ad must always have "a call to action" to show the audience what immediate step to take to engage with your product or service. This could be asking them to email, text or call with a promotional code, click a button or link to place an order or book an appointment.

9. Negotiate with advertising houses based on what you pay for readership and audience, not just on what is quoted.

10. Constantly evaluate and test the effectiveness of your ads and stop using a medium or method if it's not working. In the words of David Ogilvy, *"Never stop testing, and your advertising will never stop improving."*[63]

To be very effective with your advertising strategy, you need to consciously plan for it, choose the best methods or mediums, and constantly assess each one's effectiveness. You advertise to introduce your product or service, but the quality of your product is what brings the returns. In the final analysis, as Jef I. Richards says, *"Advertising is totally unnecessary. Unless you hope to make money."*[64]

Sales Strategy

> *"Selling is a skill to master. You will ALWAYS be selling no matter what you do."* [65]
> Karen Katz

As a new business, your commitment and enthusiasm to what you are going to sell is essential for your survival in the marketplace. Your ability to market your products and services will determine the success or failure of the business; however, for that to be possible, you must be able to sell effectively to generate revenues and profits.

A sales strategy is not the same as a marketing strategy. Your marketing strategy should enable you make yourself known to your market and get customers to be keen on what you are offering, and your sales strategy should help you "close the deal" with your customers. A sales strategy, properly implemented, should generate increased sales and enable you effectively establish yourself in the competition.

For a sales strategy to be relevant, it is important to have different sales strategies for each of your product lines, being conscious of the different customer groups or segments you will be selling to. Here are a few steps that can guide you in putting together an effective sales strategy.

Set objectives – To start with, you must have objectives for your sales strategy. These objectives must be specific, measurable, achievable, realistic, and time-sensitive (SMART). Your focus can be on specific products or client groups.

Establish features and benefits – You must also distinguish clearly the unique features of your products and services and the benefits your customers will gain from buying them. Consider the product from your customers' perspective, and emphasise the different features of the benefits.

Understand the competition – You need to also understand what your competitors are doing and how they are doing it. Evaluate their methods and establish what you can and should be doing differently.

Define your target market – A clearly defined target market is a must to enable you sell strategically to generate revenue. Constantly evaluate your customer groups or segments, and design specific strategies to use in selling your products or services to each of them.

Choose sales methods – You must now decide which sales methods to use to reach out to the various groups after identifying them and establishing the benefits your products will bring to them. The nature of product you are selling and the geographical area should also help you determine which method will best enable you get to the customer to "close a deal." Some of the sales methods to use include direct face-to-face selling, telesales, Internet, and direct mail.

Present products well – It is very important to put resources and effort into how you are going to present your products or services to your customers. There is a popular saying: *"what you see is what you get."*

Have the flexibility to negotiate – There must be a level of flexibility in your selling approach. You will need to be able to spot opportunities for the long term and be willing to cut down on your profit margin now by lowering your prices for repeat sales as well as promotional benefits.

Close the deal – This is where you persuade your customer to buy, highlighting their need or want of what you are offering. It must not stop there. You must get a firm commitment, taking note of the ensuing negotiation, listening carefully to what the customer is saying.

Follow up – Following up on the sale is a stepping-stone for creating a good rapport with a customer. Following up confirms to the customer your faith in the product and the integrity of the benefit and features you sold to them. Requesting customer feedback can give you a clear insight into the exact mindset of your customer and can also give you further ideas for improvement on your product or service.

Using Social Media For Business

The use of social media has become very prominent in marketing products and services in the last decade, and I challenge you to explore and take full advantage of it, if you are not doing that already. According to a report by WeAreSocial[66], social media users passed the 3.5 billion mark in July 2019.

Social media marketing has become a prominent medium in complementing other methods of marketing and advertising without necessarily interfering with them. The benefits can be tremendous but must be used in the most strategic and efficient way possible because almost every platform has its own unique type of audience who generally use them.

It used to be that businesses simply signed up to any of the social media platforms, such as social networking websites, blogs, or video and photo sharing platforms, and built a following over time to gain much-needed visible popularity and introduce the business to followers or subscribers.

With the constant changes in the algorithms and monetisation strategies employed by the platforms, businesses have had to constantly evolve and adapt to be able to use the platforms more effectively.

Many social networks continue to make available tools that enable users to collect detailed geographical, demographic, and personal information. This enable marketers to customise their ads.

Among the benefits of this is the ability to attract a more targeted segment of the audience, enabling you to get the necessary local and global exposure, and also helping you build a brand around your product or service.

Irrespective of the risk of fake news, scams and spam on the Internet, the major platforms, at least, continue to see growth in the number of users.

Given that practically anyone who can use the Internet can sign up to a social network website, it requires almost no special skills in its usage. Because signing up to join most of the websites and forums are free, it's one of the cheapest ways of marketing, and the return on investment, when used effectively, can be very high. This should be great news for any new and existing businesses with tight budgets.

The use of Facebook, Instagram, LinkedIn, Twitter, Pinterest, and other social networking sites to connect and interact with customers is growing in a more personalised way. As of August 2020, some of the brands with the biggest followings on various platforms include PlayStation with 18.7 million followers on Twitter, Nike with 120 million followers on Instagram, Samsung with 160 million followers on Facebook, Google with 14.9 million followers on LinkedIn and Lego with 9.77 million followers on YouTube. These are clear examples of the growing use of social networking platforms to engage and grow brands.

Followers of these and many other brands are constantly seeking knowledge about new product launches, services, special deals etc. This has reduced these brands' reliance on expensive, traditional, paid media to deliver timely deals and offers at a minimal variable cost, and has also enabled them to develop a closer relationship with their consumers.

Businesses are increasingly using social media for many reasons including monitoring conversations about its brand, and are using that to respond to consumers, analyse its reach, engagement, and traffic flow to its site with the deployment of analytics tools provided by the platforms. Businesses that want to reach a specific target audience can easily run highly targeted social media ads.

The five core pillars of social media marketing are:

1. **Strategy** – This include establishing how a platform will help you achieve your business goals. Is it to increase brand awareness, drive traffic to your website, engage consumers around your brand, create a community or serve as customer support channel for your consumers? The smartest thing to do is start with just a few platforms where your target audience can be found. You have to also decide on the type of content that will best work for you – images, videos, or links – and whether you share educational or entertaining content.
2. **Planning and publishing** – The key to the success of this is being present and consistent. Planning what to share, be it an image, video, or blog post, and on which platform is critical to your success. The content must be something your audience likes, shared at the right time and frequency. Scheduling tools such as Buffer,

Hootsuite, etc., can help you publish your content automatically at your preferred time, saving you time and enabling you to reach your audience when they are most likely to engage.
3. **Listening and engagement** – Monitoring conversations about your business or brand is especially important for growing your brand. It is an opportunity to offer support and even correct situations before they get out of hand or have a chance to respond to a positive comment. You can check all your notifications manually or use social media listening and engagement tools that help to pull in your brand mentions, messages and posts your business might not have been tagged in.
4. **Analytics** – To be effective in your social media marketing campaign it is important to check out how you are performing. This includes taking note of how many people you are reaching, how many are using your hashtags on their social media posts, how many positive mentions you get a week, month, quarter, etc. You can use the analytics tools provide on the platforms, and a wide range of external analytics tools.
5. **Advertising** – Social media ads enable you to reach a wider audience than just your followers. Targeted ads can be improved based on demographics, behaviours, interests, location, etc. The effectiveness of your ad has everything

to do with your knowledge of your audience and how to use the available tools on the platforms. That is the best way to get returns on your investment.

Using social media has basically become the online version of word-of-mouth marketing. Using it in the right way will potentially result in more customers, increased sales, great feedback, and, thus, profit, growth and continuity of the business.

10

HOW TO PUT A COMPELLING PLAN TOGETHER

> "Before everything else, getting ready is the secret of success."
> Henry Ford, a prominent American industrialist and founder of the Ford Motor Company

My experience in the field has exposed to me the level of confusion many associate with the subject of business planning. I find people who are honestly so intimidated by writing a business plan that they have never started the business they dreamt of. Others question its importance because they think it's only for securing external funding, and because they are not interested in any external funding, they decide there is no need to put one together. There are countless others who just never bothered about it. Some simply consulted their accountants or business advisors to write it for them. Unfortunately, for some members of this last group, their presentations to bankers and investors were not convincing enough to secure the needed funding.

As a principle, I only provide this service for my clients if they agree to work with me on it, especially if it is for the purpose of securing funding. That way, they get to be involved and are in the position to explain the underlying reasoning and assumptions behind the contents.

An international consultant, Dr. Graeme Edwards, once said, *"It's not the plan that is important, it's the planning."*[67] The real value of creating the business plan is not in having the finished product in hand; rather, the value lies in the process of researching and thinking about your business in a systematic way. The act of planning helps you to think things through thoroughly, study and research if you are not sure of the facts, and look at your ideas critically. A business plan is a futuristic document, and almost every point in there is based on one assumption or the other.

A business plan is simply putting together a written document that describes a business, its objectives, its strategies, the market it's in, and its financial forecasts. The process of writing a good business plan, among other things, will help put your ideas and research into a more structured format, clarify the purpose of the business, verify that the business idea is realistic and commercially viable, essentially help set sales and financial targets, plan for the future of the business, and set out the business and marketing strategies.

It has both internal and external uses. For internal purposes, it can be used to help measure success, focus on development efforts, help spot potential pitfalls before they manifest, and structure the financial aspects of a business. On the other hand, it is used externally to introduce the business to or apply for funding from bankers, external investors (friends, venture capitalist firms), grant providers, potential buyers of the business, and potential partners.

Whichever way you look at it, the business plan is simply one of the most essential pieces of documentation that any person starting a business needs to consider putting together. In the words of Chris Corrigan, an Australian businessman, *"You can't overestimate the need to plan and prepare. In most of the mistakes I've made, there has been this common theme of inadequate planning beforehand. You really can't over-prepare in business!"*[68]

Planning is key to ensuring the continuous existence of an existing business. Every business that seeks to be successful must regularly review its business plan to ensure it continues to meet its needs. It is sensible to review current performance on a regular basis and identify the most likely strategies for growth. Once you have reviewed your progress and identified the key growth areas you want to target, it's time to revisit your business plan and make it a road map to the next stages of your business.

For a new business, it is important to establish the purpose of the plan from the onset, because the emphasis of any plan should be dependent on the intended user. In the next few pages, I am going to discuss the essential components of a typical business plan. This guide, when used with my uniquely designed template (you can contact me to order your template), can help you write a compelling business plan. It will save you a lot of consultation hours. For most of my clients, I offer the template and guide, encouraging them to complete the template and bring it over for us to professionally fine-tune together for the intended purpose.

A typical plan includes:

An Executive Summary

The executive summary is an overview of the business you want to start, a synopsis of the key points of your entire plan. It should include highlights from each section of the rest of the document, from the key features of the business opportunity to the elements of the financial forecasts. It should clearly and concisely address each of the following subjects:

- Overview of the company
- Recap of the opportunity. Quantify and describe the opportunity and where you fit. Explain why you are in business, along with the reasons you will be able to take advantage of this opportunity.
- Brief summary of the market. How large is the market and what stage of development is it at (early growth versus mature)? What are the key drivers, trends, and influences in the market?
- Differentiation. What separates you from the rest of the pack? Is your product proprietary, patented, copyrighted? Is your service or product better, faster, cheaper and, if so, why? Is your advantage a temporary opportunity, and are there steps you can take to protect your position?
- Description of products or services. A very brief overview and description of your products and services.
- Management composition. It is said that investors invest in people, not products. It's a proven fact that a company's management team is one of the best predictors of success, and investors will look very closely at the individuals who will be managing the company. The ideal scenario is that

senior managers have previously started and successfully managed companies in the same business. Short of this, you want to emphasise the previous relevant experience of the management team. Names of companies and positions held, and milestones achieved are worth emphasising.
- Nature and use of proceeds. What type of funding are you looking for? Equity capital, grants, or loans? Undercapitalisation is a major cause of new start-up business failure. You should have a very clear idea of how much money you will need to operate your business for the first full year. Banks' loan officers and investors always want to know how the funds will be used. Check out my book *Pitch Your Business Like a Pro* for all the types of business funding available, etc.
- Key financials, such as forecast cash flow statement and profit and loss account, etc.

The ultimate purpose of the executive summary is to explain the basics of your business in a way that both informs and interests the reader. If, after reading the executive summary, an investor or manager understands what the business is about and is keen to know more, it has done its job.

The executive summary should be concise, no longer than two pages, and interesting. For instance, if applying for a loan, state clearly how much you want, precisely how you are going to use it, and how the money will make your business more profitable, thereby ensuring repayment. It's advisable to write the executive summary of your plan after you've completed the rest.

General Personal and Company Description

Personal details – Name, home address, telephone number, mobile phone number, date of birth, and marital status.

Business details – Business name, business address, telephone, fax, and e-mail.

Mission statement – Many companies have a brief mission statement, usually thirty words or fewer, explaining their reasons for being and their guiding principles. If you want to draft a mission statement, this is a good place to put it in the plan.

Company goals and objectives – Goals are destinations. Objectives are progress markers along the way to goal achievement.

Business philosophy – What is important to you in business?

To whom will you market your products? State it briefly here – it should be dealt with more thorough in the *Marketing Plan* section.

Describe your industry – Is it a growth industry? What changes do you foresee in the industry, short-term and long-term? How will your company be poised to take advantage of them?

Describe your most important company strengths and core competencies. What factors will make the company succeed? What do you think your major competitive strengths will be? What background experience, skills, and strengths do you personally bring to this new venture?

Legal form of ownership – Sole Proprietor, partnership, corporation, Limited Liability Company or corporation? Why have you selected this form?

Exit strategy – You may want to explain to investors how they will get their money back, what you are anticipating they will recover in excess of their investment, and in what time frame. Possible exit strategies can include the sale or merger of your company, a management buyout, an IPO, or a private placement.

Products and Services

Describe your products or services in depth. Technical specifications, drawings, photos, sales brochures, and other bulky items belong in *Appendices*. Discuss pricing, service, support, warranty, production, etc.

What are the advantages of your products or services, and how do they compare to the competition? Examples include level of quality or unique or distinguishing features. What is the timetable for introducing these products, and what steps need to be taken to ensure this timeline is met? Are there other vendors involved, and if so, who, and where do they fit? Have your products been tested or evaluated, and if so, where, when, and what were the results? Are there plans for future or next-generation products, and if so, what and when? Are these new products included in your revenue and cost projections?

Marketing Plan

RESEARCH

Why? It is quite deceptive to assume that you already know about your intended market. You need to do market research to make sure you are on track. Use the opportunity to uncover data and to question your marketing efforts.

How? There are two kinds of market research: primary and secondary.

Primary research means gathering your own data.

Secondary research means using published information, such as industry profiles, trade journals, newspapers, magazines, census data, and demographic profiles. This type of information is available in public libraries, industry associations, chambers of commerce, from vendors who sell to your industry, and from government agencies.

In your marketing plan, be as specific as possible: give statistics, numbers, and sources. The marketing plan will be the basis later on of all important sales projections.

Facts about your industry:

- What is the total size of your market?
- What percentage share of the market will you have?
- Current demand in target market
- Trends in target market – growth trends, trends in consumer preferences, and trends in product development
- Growth potential and opportunity for a business of your size

What barriers to entry do you face in entering this market with your new company? Some typical barriers may include:

- High capital costs
- High production costs
- High marketing costs
- Consumer acceptance and brand recognition
- Training and skills
- Unique technology and patents
- Unions
- Shipping costs
- Tariff barriers and quotas

How will you overcome the barriers? How could the following affect your company?

- Changes in technology
- Changes in government regulations
- Changes in the economy
- Changes in your industry

PRODUCTS

In the *Products and Services* section, you described your products and services as you see them. Now, describe them from your customers' points of view.

Features and benefits – List all of your major products or services.

For each product or service:

- Describe the most important features. What is special about it?
- Describe the benefits. That is, what will the product do for the customer?

Note the difference between features and benefits, and think about them. For example, a house that gives shelter and lasts a long time is made with certain materials and to a certain design; those are its features. Its benefits include pride of ownership, financial security, providing for the family, and inclusion in a neighbourhood. You build features into your product so that you can sell the benefits.

What after-sale services will you give? Some examples are delivery, warranty, service contracts, support, follow-up, and refunds.

CUSTOMERS

Identify your targeted customers, their characteristics, and their geographic locations, i.e., their demographics. The description will be completely different depending on whether you plan to sell to other businesses or directly to consumers. Then, for each customer group, construct what is called a demographic profile, including age, gender, location, income level, social class, occupation, and education level. For business customers, the demographic factors might be industry, location, size of firm, quality, technology, and price preferences.

COMPETITION

What products and companies will compete with you? List your major competitors (names and addresses). Will they compete with you across the board, or just for certain products, certain customers, or in certain locations?

Will you have important indirect competitors? For example, video rental stores compete with theatres, although they are different types of businesses. How will your products or services compare with the competition?

Other areas to consider: niche, marketing strategy, promotion, promotional budget, pricing (explain your methods of setting prices), proposed location, and distribution channels (how you sell your products or services: retail, direct mail order, website, catalogue, wholesale, your own sales force, agents, independent representatives, bid on contracts).

SALES FORECAST

It's time to attach some numbers to your plan. Use a sales forecast spreadsheet to prepare a month-by-month projection. The forecast should be based on your historical sales, the marketing strategies you have just described in your market research, and industry data, if available.

You may want to do two forecasts:

1) A "best guess," which is what you really expect.
2) A "worst case" low estimate that you are confident you can reach no matter what happens.

Remember to keep notes on your research and your assumptions as you build this sales forecast and all subsequent spreadsheets in the plan. This is critical if you are going to present it to funding sources.

SWOT ANALYSIS

A SWOT analysis simply helps you to assess your *Strengths* and *Weaknesses*, and the *Opportunities* and *Threats* your business faces or may face in the course of operations. It provides a clear basis for examining your business performance and prospects.

There are various ways by which you can assess your *strengths*. Continual dialogue with customers or potential customers and suppliers may provide a clue as to where your strengths are. Rising sales, for an existing business, in a particular product, a strong balance sheet, positive cash flow, growing turnover and profitability, skilled financial management, skilled employees, successful recruitment, effective training and development, modern, low-cost production facilities, a good location, market leadership in a profitable niche, an established customer base, a strong product range, effective research and development, a skilled sales team, and thorough after-sales service, are all good indicators.

Weaknesses, on the other hand, can be known through various indicators, most of which are the opposite of the strength of the business. They are usually known but tend to be ignored. Not having the right financial management expert or system in place will result in poor credit control, leading to unpredictable cash flow or insufficient funds unavailable for investment. Others may be a limited or outdated product range, complacency and failure to innovate, over-reliance on a few customers, expertise and control locked up in a few key personnel, high staff turnover, long leases tying the business to unsuitable premises or equipment, inefficient processes, outdated equipment, high cost of production, and low productivity.

Changes in the business's external environment can provide great *opportunities*, which, when well managed, can be turned into an advantage for the business. External factors include things such as improved access to potential new customers and markets overseas, the development of new distribution channels such as the Internet, deterioration in a competitor's performance or the insolvency of a competitor, securing financiers to fund expansion, which could be a result of political, legislative, or regulatory changes, economic trends such as a fall in interest rates, introduction of new technology for a process, increased sales to existing customers or new leads gained through them, and social developments such as demographic changes.

Threats can be major or minor. Even minor threats can have far-reaching consequences on the business, destroying its survival and profitability. These could be in the form of loss of a significant customer, price rises from suppliers, lenders reducing credit lines or increasing charges, improved competitive products or the emergence of new competitors, key personnel leaving, perhaps with trade secrets, new technology that makes your products obsolete or gives competitors an advantage, legal action taken against you by a customer, social developments such as consumer demands for environmentally friendly or ethics-based products, political, legislative, and regulatory changes such as new regulations increasing your costs or requiring product redesign.

The results of SWOT analyses should not be the end but rather a starting point. You can capitalise on the results and play to your strengths, as each business is different. Opportunities that are in line with your strengths may prompt you to pursue a strategy of aggressive expansion.

You should prioritise the weaknesses and address those that can be addressed. Weaknesses that cannot be addressed now must be acknowledged and respected until time and resources allow a solution. Some weaknesses can be turned into strengths or opportunities, such as turning a shortage of production capacity into scarcity value for your product. Other weaknesses, such as financial ones, might be solved by raising further funds, or management shortcomings solved by recruiting new personnel. Some will need a significant investment in time and resources. You may for instance, need to start a program of improvements through training or quality management. The analysis could also suggest other strategic options for the business, such as taking defensive measures in areas of threat where weakness had been identified or diversifying away from areas of significant threat to more promising opportunities.

Some of the ways of protecting your business against threats include fostering good employee relations, taking out insurance cover against obvious potential disasters, investing in legal protection for your intellectual property, taking advantage of low fixed interest rates to move your overdraft to long-term loans, ensuring you have clear and reasonable contracts with suppliers, customers, and employees, building relationships with suppliers and customers, drawing up realistic contingency plans to cope with potential crises, and introducing the right types of service contracts for key personnel.

Operational Plan

Explain the daily operation of the business, its location, equipment, people, processes, and surrounding environment.

Production – How and where are your products or services produced?

Location – What qualities do you need in a location? Describe the type of location you'll have.

Legal environment – licensing and bonding requirements, permits, health, workplace, or environmental regulations, special regulations covering your industry or profession, etc.

Personnel – number of employees, type of labour, where you find the right employees, quality of existing staff, pay structure, training methods and requirements, task breakdown, etc.

Inventory – What kind of inventory will you keep: raw materials, supplies, finished goods? Average value in stock (i.e., what is your inventory investment). Rate of turnover and how this compares to the industry averages. Seasonal build-ups. Lead time for ordering.

Suppliers – Identify key suppliers, with names and addresses, type and amount of inventory furnished, credit and delivery policies, history, and reliability.

Credit policies – Do you plan to sell on credit? Do you really need to sell on credit? Is it customary in your industry and expected by your clientele? If yes, what policies will you have about who gets credit and how much? How will you check the creditworthiness of new applicants? What terms will you offer your customer – that is, how much credit, and when will payment be due?

Managing your accounts receivable – If you do extend credit, you should do an aging report at least monthly. (An aging report is a list of customers' accounts receivable amounts by how long they are owed.) This will help you track how much of your money is tied up in credit given to customers, and will alert you to slow payment problems.

Managing your accounts payable – You should also age your accounts payable, what you owe to your suppliers. This helps you plan whom to pay and when. Paying too early depletes your cash, but paying late can cost you valuable discounts and can damage your credit.

Management and Organisation Plan

Who will manage the business on a day-to-day basis? What experience does that person bring to the business? What special or distinctive competencies does he or she have? Is there a plan for continuation of the business if this person is lost or incapacitated?

The section should go into some detail about the individuals who will be entrusted with the investors' money. Stress relevant experience and previous success. This section of the plan should include:

- Biographic summary of key management
- Organisational charts (current and future)
- Manpower table
- Board of advisors
- Board of directors

If you'll have more than ten employees, create an organisational chart showing the management hierarchy and who is responsible for key functions. Include position descriptions for key employees. If you are seeking loans or investors, include resumes (in the *Appendices*) of owners and key employees.

Professional and Advisory Support

List the following:

- Board of directors
- Management advisory board
- Attorney
- Accountant
- Insurance agent

Personal Financial Statement

Include personal financial statements for each owner and major stockholder, showing assets and liabilities held outside the business and personal net worth. Owners will often have to draw on personal assets to finance the business, and these statements will show what is available. Bankers and investors usually want this information as well.

It is also important that thought goes into the amount of money you require per month to maintain your current standard of living, let alone improve it. The business needs to know how much you require so that pricing decisions can be realistically made.

Start-Up Expenses and Capitalisation

You will have quite a number of expenses before you even begin operating your business. It's important to estimate these expenses accurately and plan where you will get sufficient capital from. Remember, this will include the money for buying or leasing premises, making those premises suitable for your business (even if working from home, you may need to convert a room into an office), any equipment you may need, and working money to get you through those first lean months as the business becomes established.

Some of the quick questions that need to be realistically answered are:

- Where will I get the money that I need to start up my business?
- Do I have money of my own?
- Can my family and friends help me?
- Do I qualify for an existing government grant or scheme?
- Is a loan from the bank my best option?
- What will the interest rate be?

The more thorough your research efforts, the less chance you will leave out important expenses or underestimate them. A rule of thumb is that contingencies should equal at least 20% of the total of all other start-up expenses.

Explain your research and how you arrived at your forecasts of expenses. Give sources, amounts, and terms of proposed loans. Also explain in detail how much will be contributed by each investor and what percent ownership each will have. A sample Set-Up Cost page can be found as Appendix I.

Financial Plan

The financial plan may consist of twelve months' or one to five years' profit and loss projection, a cash-flow projection, a projected balance sheet, and a break-even calculation. Together, they constitute a reasonable estimate of your company's financial future. More importantly, the process of thinking through the financial plan will improve your insight into the inner financial workings of your company.

Projected cash flow – If the profit projection is the heart of your business plan, cash flow is the blood. Businesses fail because they cannot pay their bills. Every part of your business plan is important, but none of it means a thing if you run out of cash. A sample Forecast Cash Flow Statement can be found as Appendix II.

Profit and loss statement – The primary tool for good financial reporting is the profit and loss statement. This is a measure of a company's sales and expenses over a specific period of time. It is prepared at regular intervals (monthly for the first year and annually through five years) to show the results of operating during those accounting periods. It should follow generally accepted accounting principles and must contain specific revenue and expense categories, regardless of the nature of the business. A sample Forecast Profit and Loss Statement can be found as Appendix III.

Opening day balance sheet – A balance sheet is one of the fundamental financial reports that any business needs for reporting and financial management. A balance sheet shows what items of value are held by the company (assets) and what its debts are (liabilities). When liabilities are subtracted from assets, the remainder is owners' equity. A sample Forecast Balance Sheet Statement can be found as Appendix IV.

Break-even analysis – A break-even analysis predicts the sales volume, at a given price, required to recover total costs.

The sales level is the dividing line between operating at a loss and operating at a profit. Expressed as a formula, break-even is:

$$\text{Breakeven Sales} = \frac{\text{Fixed Costs}}{1 - \text{Variable Costs}}$$

where fixed costs are expressed in dollars, but variable costs are expressed as a percentage of total sales.

Everything you've included in the plan up to this point should support your financial assumptions and projections. In other words, the reader shouldn't be surprised when they see your three-to-five-year revenue forecast because you've given them detailed information on the market, the opportunity, and your strategies. You've described the advantages that you have over the competition; you have outlined how you plan to reach the market, and the management team you have to help you achieve your objectives. Your projections should represent a logical conclusion to everything you've included in the plan.

Finally, as Ronald Reagan said, *"Each generation goes further than the generation preceding it because it stands on the shoulders of that generation. You will have opportunities beyond anything we have ever known."* Francis Bacon, Sr., said, *"The wise man will make more opportunities than he finds."* And, in the words of Robert Schuller, *"High achievers spot rich opportunities swiftly, make big decisions quickly and move into action immediately. Follow these principles and you can make your dreams come true."*[69]

Appendices

Include details and studies in your business plan. For example, include:

- Brochures and advertising materials
- Industry reports and information
- Forecasted profit and loss statement
- Forecasted cash flow statement
- Blueprints and plans, maps and photos of location(s)
- Magazine articles or other relevant articles
- Detailed lists of equipment owned or to be purchased
- Copies of leases and contracts
- Letters of support from future customers
- Any other materials needed to support the assumptions in this plan
- Market research studies
- List of assets available as collateral for a loan

Fine-Tuning the Plan for an Intended User

The generic business plan presented above should be modified to suit your specific type of business and the audience for which the plan is written.

For Raising Capital

For bankers – Bankers want assurance of orderly repayment. If you intend using this plan to present to lenders, include:

- The amount of the loan and how the funds will be used, what the funds will accomplish and how they will make the business stronger
- Requested repayment terms (number of years to repay). You will probably not have much negotiating room on interest rate but may be able to negotiate a longer repayment term, which will help cash flow.
- Collateral offered, and a list of all existing liens against collateral

For investors – Investors have a different perspective. They are looking for dramatic growth, and they expect to share in the rewards. Include information about:

- Funds needed short-term
- Funds needed in two to five years
- How the company will use the funds, and what this will accomplish in terms of growth
- Estimated return on investment
- Exit strategy for investors (buyback, sale, or IPO)
- Percent of ownership you will give up to investors
- Milestones or conditions you will accept

- Financial reporting to be provided
- Involvement of investors on the board or in management

As comprehensive as this guide may be, the time and resources you invest in putting it together is very important for achieving the right result. Whether it is for internal or external use, you owe it to yourself to establish the underlying assumptions that are realistic and consistent with the industry of your choice.

> *"You are the embodiment of the information you choose to accept and act upon. To change your circumstances, you need to change your thinking and subsequent actions."*[70]
> Adlin Sinclair.

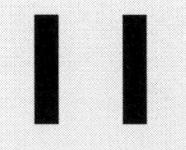

QUALITIES OF SUCCESSFUL BUSINESSPEOPLE

> *"Whenever an individual or a business decides that success has been attained, progress stops."*
> Thomas J. Watson, *former President of International Business Machines (IBM), who developed IBM's renowned management style and corporate culture*

I have yet to come across a person in business who does not aspire to succeed in his or her chosen business. However, the desire to succeed is not a guarantee to becoming successful. There are certain characteristics and attitudes that distinguish those who have succeeded from those who are simply surviving. Not possessing any of these qualities does not in any way disqualify you from starting out. I believe most of these qualities can be developed over time should you set your mind to it. Choices, not circumstances, determine your success. Here are some of the qualities for your consideration.

Desire – To succeed, you have to have an above-average desire to break out of the 9 to 5 grind, to step off the employee-job-salary treadmill, and to put your ideas, ideals, and beliefs into action.

Eric Hoffer stated, *"It sometimes seems that intense desire creates not only its own opportunities, but its own talents."*[71] An entrepreneur's desire for personal fulfilment and professional success is his or her number one key strength and that which will force him or her to start out in business in the first place. In the words of Napoleon Hill, *"When your desires are strong enough, you will appear to possess superhuman powers to achieve."*[72] Success can only be yours if you desire enough to act to achieve it.

Passion – To be successful in business, you need to be passionate in what you are doing or intend to do. John Maxwell said, *"A great leader's courage to fulfil his vision comes from passion, not position."*[73] Passion generates energy and excitement for the task ahead. Setting out to go into business on your own is a great decision but can be challenging, especially in the initial stages. Unless you are passionate about what you have on offer, you may not get anyone to want to pay for it, let alone survive to succeed in it.

Purpose – Successful businesspeople have a definite purpose or goal in life, know what they want, and pursue it until they get it.

Decision-making skills – Peter Drucker once said, *"Making good decisions is a crucial skill at every level."* However, successful businesspeople take this to another level by being able to make quick decisions when it's required and sticking by those decisions. Most of these decisions are made not only based on facts but also based on what they believe in or with their instincts.

Creative imagination – Successful businesspeople are always creatively imagining scenarios and events well ahead of time. They always seek to have a peek into the future for ideas and solutions.

Leadership abilities – To be successful is equal to being able to lead yourself and others to fulfilling a desired dream or goal. A leader leads by example, whether intentionally or not. John Maxwell, a leadership expert, speaker and author, said, *"A leader is one who knows the way, goes the way, and shows the way."*[74] Also, in the words of John Quincy Adams, *"If your actions inspire others to dream more, learn more, do more and become more, you are a leader."*

Self-starters – To be successful in business, you need to have the ability to take the initiative and work independently to develop your ideas. Often, even the closest of friends and family may not see what you are seeing. Do not wait on their approval and support before you set off because it may never come. People jump on board only when they see you start.

Higher goals – Successful businesspeople are mountain climbers who, having climbed one peak, look beyond to the next highest. They are resourceful and proactive. Rather than adopting a passive "wait and see" approach, they constantly set higher goals.

Self-determination – Successful people have a strong determination to make things happen. A successful businessperson has the belief that the outcome of events is down to his or her own actions, rather than external factors or other people's actions.

Judgment – To succeed in business, you need to be openminded when listening to other people's advice, while bearing in mind your objectives for the business. You should have the ability to listen to other people's ideas without feeling intimidated or threatened.

Self-confidence – As a successful businessperson, you will need to have self-belief and passion about your product or service. Your enthusiasm should win people over to your ideas.

Seek solutions in the face of problem – Successful businesspeople are always looking at problems and challenges with the view of solving them instead of complaining about them or blaming others. They aim at solving problems rather than placing blame.

Commitment – Successful people are willing to make personal sacrifices through long hours and loss of leisure time. They are unfailingly committed and reliable to whatever they are doing. They can be counted on to get the job done and always make a positive contribution.

Patience – A very interesting quality of successful businesspeople, irrespective of their swiftness in judgment and decision making, is that they tend to know when to wait and vice versa. Patience and commitment go hand in hand, and the patient businesspeople who dedicate themselves to working away at their business day after day reap the rewards of their patience.

Realistic expectations – Ralph Marston once said, *"Don't lower your expectations to meet your performance. Raise your level of performance to meet your expectations."*[75] However, to be successful, you will have to keep your expectations realistic. It is one of the best ways to keep from getting frustrated when things don't happen as quickly as you'd like them to.

Risk – Another quality of successful people is their relentless desire for risk. Treading where no one has trod before and taking up challenges others would run away from or simply complain at.

Perseverance – The ability to continue despite setbacks, financial insecurity, and exposure to risk is necessary. Successful people move toward the pictures they create in their minds. They rehearse coming actions or events as they "see" them and persevere until that picture becomes real.

Personal and professional integrity – Having a keen sense of integrity is important to ensure that business transactions are conducted with ethics in mind. Don Galer said, "*Integrity is what we do, what we say, and what we say we do.*"[76] A successful businessperson conducts him or herself in a respectable manner and always acts fairly and responsibly. Richard Buckminster Fuller stated, "*Integrity is the essence of everything successful.*"[77] Those who ignored this principle later regretted it when all they built crumbled right before them after being found out.

Driven by accomplishments, not money – Successful businesspeople follow the theory of Apple Inc.'s founder, Steve Jobs, who said, *"The journey is the reward."* They are customer-focused, not product-focused.

Negotiators – You have to be good or develop the ability to negotiate skilfully to make it in business. Howard Baker explains that *"the most difficult thing in any negotiation, almost, is making sure that you strip it of the emotion and deal with the facts."*[78] Almost every business transaction has to be negotiated to get it signed off. In the words of Chester Karrass, *"In business, you don't get what you deserve, you get what you negotiate for."*

Time management – Your ability to manage time is a key to being successful, not only in business but in life. Peter Drucker said, *"Time is the scarcest resource and unless it is managed nothing else can be managed."*[79]

Succeeding in business is more than buying and selling products. All the above qualities as well as some that were not mentioned can go a long way to influencing a businessperson's ability to manage a business of any size at any level and still succeed, ensuring growth and profitability.

12

CONCLUSION

> "When written in Chinese, the word 'crisis' is composed of two characters – one represents danger and the other represents opportunity."
> John F. Kennedy, 35th President of the United States

In conclusion, in the midst of the pandemic, with its associated economic downturn and uncertainty, there are many who have found the way to lift their heads above the storm. Most of these people, I believe, may not have necessarily planned to do so. However, the challenges of the times and life have a very interesting way of squeezing the creativity out of us, if not for anything more than the survival instinct in man.

Jonathan Schattke said, *"Necessity is the mother of invention, it is true, but its father is creativity, and knowledge is the midwife."*[80] By this book I have presented a significant amount of knowledge to help you to innovate and create new businesses. And at times, as Brian Koslow said, *"the freedom to move forward to new opportunities and to produce results comes from living in the present not the past."* [81]

The times we are in are undoubtedly some of the most challenging, as well as the best times, that is, only if you decide to look at it the other way around. Many have taken advantage of the opportunities staring right up in their faces. New wealth is being created with fresh millionaires being made each day. At the same time, businesses are closing their doors and others are giving up, while their competitors are seizing the opportunities.

The ability to seize opportunities by connecting problems and questions with solutions and answers, and turning them into viable money-making business ventures is one of the most creative things any individual can do to become part of the new wealth creators. Mary Lou Cook, an American educationist, once said, *"Creativity is inventing, experimenting, growing, taking risks, breaking rules, making mistakes, and having fun."* [82]

Interestingly, opportunities do not often show up with labels and signposts. The big ones we tend to wish for and daydream about seldom come by, and if any turn up, chances of accessing them and owning them are very slim. Experienced surfers will tell you that waiting for the big wave can take a very long while, and when it comes, you might only have one shot at it because even *"ability is of little account without opportunity"* – Napoleon. Jumping at several smaller opportunities daily has proven over time to be the better prospect.

If you ignore a chance, someone else will surely find it. Unfortunately, they will be the ones to enjoy the fruits should the idea succeed. Being creative as you go about your daily activities and engaging your brain can help you solve almost every problem there is in life. And you will be glad to know that life only pays you for the problems you solve. Woody Allen, an American screenwriter, director, and author, sums it up this way, *"It is clear the future holds great opportunities. It also holds pitfalls. The trick will be to avoid the pitfalls, seize the opportunities, and get back home by six o'clock."*[83]

To have an upper hand over the economic uncertainties as you start and grow your business:

- Set specific objectives and plan your days around what you need to get done to generate income.

- Learn to focus on what you are best at to make your products and services better, and let others handle aspects you are least capable of handling. Adding value to your products and services tends to be far more appealing to customers than just lowering prices.

- Stick to the line of business you are passionate about and more able to survive the times with. That is, if you have other lines of business, expand existing lines that are doing well. Look at the competition, rename, repackage, and re-price your products, offering multiple price options to the customer. Customers are more likely to choose among the options you are offering instead of looking for alternative sellers.

- Better still, develop products and services that address the current market needs and are able to generate the quickest income. Or develop a niche product for a segment of your market that is more resilient in the face of the changes in the economy. Or identify a new market, plan, and access it.

- Manage cash wisely. Like they say, "cash is king." Lower cash flow can potentially suck the life out of the business. Make every effort to search for and take advantage of trade offers and discounts to free up cash. Even if you have to borrow, revisit your assumptions in line with current economic conditions. Otherwise, work at decreasing expenditure (such as taking advantage of webinars to cut down travel cost) and increase cash revenue (less selling on credit) with the aim to increase profits with time.

- Review your business and marketing plan and make the necessary changes to reflect the direction of the market with an eye on the marketing expenses. Adopt new strategies to address the changes. You may, for instance, need to re-evaluate your pricing strategy and decide to offer discounts on your most popular products and services.

- If there is any time to give more attention to existing and past customers, it is now. Reach out more to them, reminding them of your continued business with them. Make cash rewards and gift incentives available in exchange for referrals from them.

- It is also a great time to evaluate your procedures and operational policies and make them relevant to the current market conditions and customer needs. Use customer surveys and feedback, and ask basic questions such as:
  - Are customer services teams providing the best service?
  - Do the sales teams need new training?

- Are there any ways to improve performance and growth? What are they?

- A time of laxity in business is a great opportunity to expand your knowledge base by taking up new courses, reading new books, networking with others in the industry, getting involved in trade associations, and even seeking joint ventures and partnerships.

- Do everything to study and understand the market; specifically how your products and services are affected by the changes in the economy. Use this knowledge to build on your competitive advantage.

Starting and growing a business that survives the economic downturn is a sure recipe for succeeding in the good economic times. That is exactly what this book offers you: an opportunity to look at the economic downturn differently and take advantage of the great opportunities it presents as you seek to earn income or extra income, or to fulfil a dream and become part of the breed of new wealth creators.

Step-by-Step Checklist

Here's a quick rundown of the basic steps to starting and growing a business.

1. Have a clear idea of:
   a. Product or service. What your USP (Unique Selling Point) will be. Be **passionate** about it.
   b. Branding. Choose a name, logo, and slogan consistent with your aim and target audience. Ensure quality designs of letterhead, business cards, etc.
   c. Your target group.
   d. Market research.

2. Develop the idea with the customer in mind, as well as yourself and your ability to compete.

3. Decide on the business model. Office, home-based, licensing, multi-level marketing, drop shipping?

4. Decide where to start from: part time or full time?

5. Decide how you will produce the product or supply the service.

6. Check out any regulations and licenses involved.

7. Decide how much to charge for your product or service.

8. Decide how to market and sell your product or service: online, direct mail, telemarketing, designing and printing (flyers, brochures, etc.), exhibitions, websites, research, surveys, promotions, press releases, public relations, photography, and advertising.

9. Decide the legal structure (Sole Trader, partnership, Limited Liability Company, etc.) that will favour you. Register the business where necessary. Resolve who will manage the business.

10. Decide on your capital requirements and how to fund them. It will be in your interest to prepare a cash flow and profit and loss forecast for twelve months, or one to five years, or both.

11. Get to know basic information about taxes, National Insurance, salaries and wages, and business rates.

12. Do everything possible to put your business plan together, either as a formal document or in any informal way you choose to write it.

Thank you for ordering a copy of this book, and I hope you have or are about to take the necessary steps to start out. If you want to be like those who have stayed above the economic storms, then follow the steps I have laid out in this book to stay atop. According to Geri Weitzman, an American author and psychologist, *"Sometimes you gotta create what you want to be a part of."* Go for it, and you will succeed one way or the other.

End of My Writing, Starting Point for Your Action

APPENDIX I

Set-up costs

Setting Up the Business
Business Consultancy/Advisory Services Fees
Business Registration
Business Logo, Letterhead, Business Cards
Domain Name Registration & Website Design
Licences
Solicitor's Fees
Insurance Premiums
Workers Compensation

Setting Up the Premises
Lease Deposit and Advance Rent
Business Rates
Fittings & Refurbishment
Utility - Water, Light, Heating
Stationery and Office Supplies

Plant and Equipment
Equipment
Vehicles
Telecommunications
Computers and Software

Starting Operations
Advertising and Promotion
Raw Materials and Supplies
Working Capital

APPENDIX II

XYZ LTD YEAR 1 CASHFLOW

	Pre-Startup £	Month 1 £	Month 2 £	Month 3 £	Month 4 £	Month 5 £	Month 6 £	Month 7 £	Month 8 £	Month 9 £	Month 10 £	Month 11 £	Month 12 £	Total £
Receipts														
Owners' Capital	0													
Bank Loan / Cash Injection		0												0
Sales		0												0
Government Grant		0												0
Total Cash Rcpts	0	0	0	0	0	0	0	0	0	0	0	0	0	
OVERHEADS														
Purchases		0	0	0	0	0	0	0	0	0	0	0	0	0
Salaries		0	0	0	0	0	0	0	0	0	0	0	0	0
Emp National Insurance		0	0	0	0	0	0	0	0	0	0	0	0	0
Office Expenses		0	0	0	0	0	0	0	0	0	0	0	0	0
Rent		0	0	0	0	0	0	0	0	0	0	0	0	0
Telephone		0	0	0	0	0	0	0	0	0	0	0	0	0
Business Rate		0	0	0	0	0	0	0	0	0	0	0	0	0
Water Rates		0	0	0	0	0	0	0	0	0	0	0	0	0
Subscription		0	0	0	0	0	0	0	0	0	0	0	0	0
Bank Charges & Interest		0	0	0	0	0	0	0	0	0	0	0	0	0
General Expenses		0	0	0	0	0	0	0	0	0	0	0	0	0
Training & Development		0	0	0	0	0	0	0	0	0	0	0	0	0
Heating & Lighting		0	0	0	0	0	0	0	0	0	0	0	0	0
Insurance		0	0	0	0	0	0	0	0	0	0	0	0	0
Loan Repayment		0	0	0	0	0	0	0	0	0	0	0	0	0
Marketing		0	0	0	0	0	0	0	0	0	0	0	0	0
Advertising		0	0	0	0	0	0	0	0	0	0	0	0	0
Professional Fees		0	0	0	0	0	0	0	0	0	0	0	0	0
Delivery Charges		0	0	0	0	0	0	0	0	0	0	0	0	0
Travel Expenses		0	0	0	0	0	0	0	0	0	0	0	0	0
Vehicle Running Cost		0	0	0	0	0	0	0	0	0	0	0	0	0
General Maintenance		0	0	0	0	0	0	0	0	0	0	0	0	0
Registration Fees	0													
Professional Fees	0													
Capital Equipment	0													
Fixtures & Fittings	0													
Stock	0													
Market Research	0													
Marketing	0													
Refurbishment	0													
Total Overheads	0	0	0	0	0	0	0	0	0	0	0	0	0	0
Monthly Cash Flow		0	0	0	0	0	0	0	0	0	0	0	0	0
Opening Bal	0	0	0	0	0	0	0	0	0	0	0	0	0	
Closing Bal	0	0	0	0	0	0	0	0	0	0	0	0	0	

APPENDIX III

XYZ LTD. YEAR 1 PROJECTED PROFIT & LOSS ACCOUNT	
	$
Sales	0
Cost/Goods Sold (COGS)	-
Gross Profit	0
Less Overheads	
Salaries	-
Emp National Insurance	-
Office Expenses	-
Rent	-
Telephone	-
Business Rate	
Water Rate	-
Subscription	-
Bank Charges and Interest	-
General Expenses	-
Training & Development	-
Heat and Light	-
Insurance	-
Loan Repayment	-
Marketing	
Advertising	-
Accounting and Legal Fees	-
Delivery Charges	-
Travel Expenses	
Vehicle Running Cost	-
General Repairs & Maintenance	-
Taxes	-
Depreciation Furniture	-
Depreciation on Equipment	-
Depreciation on Vehicle	-
Other Expense (specify)	-
	0
Net Profit before Tax	0

APPENDIX IV

Balance Sheet Forecast
As at December 20___

Assets

Current assets	£0
Cash	
Petty cash	
Accounts receivable	
Stock	
Short-term investment	
Prepaid expenses	
Long-term investment	

Fixed assets	£0
Land	
Buildings	
Improvements	
Equipment	
Furniture	
Motor vehicles	

Total assets	**£0**

Liabilities

Current liabilities	£0
Accounts payable	
Interest payable	
Taxes payable	
Income tax	
Sales tax	
Payroll accrual	

Long-term liabilities	£0
Borrowings	

Total liabilities	**£0**
Net assets	**£0**

Owner's equity

Retained earnings	
Current year earnings	£0
Total equity (should equal net assets)	**£0**

REFERENCES

1. Kaur, A & Krishna, B, 2020, *Fact Check: Jack Ma Never Said 2020 is the year of just staying alive*, India Today, viewed 13 August 2020 <https://www.indiatoday.in/fact-check/story/fact-check-jack-ma-never-said-2020-is-the-year-of-just-staying-alive-1678557-2020-05-15>

2. Arnold, M, 2020, *Slowdown in EU job losses defies economists' predictions*, Financial Times, viewed 13 August 2020 <https://www.ft.com/content/dfb83116-8dee-4374-a8fd-b04f16a03e48>

3. Kaur, A & Krishna, B, 2020, *Fact Check: Jack Ma Never Said 2020 is the year of just staying alive*, India Today, viewed 13 August 2020 <https://www.indiatoday.in/fact-check/story/fact-check-jack-ma-never-said-2020-is-the-year-of-just-staying-alive-1678557-2020-05-15>

4. Davis, Ian 2009, *The new normal*, McKinsey Quarterly, viewed 13 August 2020 <https://www.mckinsey.com/business-functions/strategy-and-corporate-finance/our-insights/the-new-normal#>

5. Americans for Tax Fairness, 2020, *Tale of Two Crises: Billionaires Gain as Workers Feel Pandemic Pain*, viewed 13 August 2020 <https://americansfortaxfairness.org/tale-two-crises-billionaires-gain-workers-feel-pandemic-pain/>

6. Bloomberg, 2020, *Bloomberg Billionaires Index*, viewed 13 August 2020 <https://www.bloomberg.com/billionaires/>

7. The World Bank, 2020, *The Global Economic Outlook During the Covid-19 Pandemic: A Changed World,* viewed 13 August 2020 <https://www.worldbank.org/en/news/feature/2020/06/08/the-global-economic-outlook-during-the-covid-19-pandemic-a-changed-world>

8. Pickard, J & Thomas, D, 2020, *Manufacturers warn of UK 'jobs bloodbath',* Financial Times, viewed 13 August 2020 <https://www.ft.com/content/afa20d03-480a-4e56-a23e-4c522d96089c>

9. Creative Industries Federation, 2020, *The Projected Economic Impact of Covid-19 on the UK Creative Industries report,* viewed 13 August 2020 <https://www.creativeindustriesfederation.com/news/press-release-cultural-catastrophe-over-400000-creative-jobs-could-be-lost-projected-economic>

10. Chan, SP, 2020, *Coronavirus: Bank pumps £100bn into UK economy to aid recovery,* BBC News, viewed 13 August 2020 <https://www.bbc.co.uk/news/uk-53093127>

11. Asian Development Bank, 2020, *COVID-19 Economic Impact Assessment Template,* viewed 13 August 2020 <https://data.adb.org/dataset/covid-19-economic-impact-assessment-template>

12. Gregory, M, 2020, *UK economy likely to take time to fully recover from coronavirus hit,* EY UK, viewed 13 August 2020 <https://www.ey.com/en_uk/growth/ey-item-club/uk-economy-likely-to-take-time-to-fully-recover-from-coronavirus-hit>

13. Insider.co.uk, 2020, *One in five small businesses adopt new technology during lockdown , finds FSB,* viewed 13 August 2020 <https://www.insider.co.uk/news/one-five-small-businesses-adopt-22179852>

Charles Swindoll title quote: Goodreads.com, 2010, *Charles R. Swindoll Quotable Quote,* viewed 13 August 2020 <https://www.goodreads.com/quotes/313428-we-are-all-faced-with-a-series-of-great-opportunities>

14. Krouse, S, 2020, *Verizon Buys Zoom Conferencing Rival BlueJeans*, The Wall Street Journal, viewed 13 August 2020 <https://www.wsj.com/articles/verizon-to-buy-zoom-conferencing-rival-bluejeans-11587041218>

15. Plummer, R, 2020, *Coronavirus: Five firms booming despite the lockdown*, BBC News, viewed 13 August 2020 <https://www.bbc.co.uk/news/business-52383193>

16. Plummer, R, 2020, *Coronavirus: Five firms booming despite the lockdown*, BBC News, viewed 13 August 2020 <https://www.bbc.co.uk/news/business-52383193>

17. Valinsky, J, 2020, *Business is booming for these 14 companies during the Coronavirus pandemic,* KQ2.com, viewed 13 August 2020 <https://www.kq2.com/content/national/570270092.html>

18. Basul, A, 2020 *85,000 online businesses launched during lockdown in the UK,* UKTN, viewed 13 August 2020 <https://www.uktech.news/news/85000-businesses-launch-online-shops-as-lockdown-creates-digital-economy-boom-20200703>

19. Yin, S, 2020, *Start-Up Activity Now HIGHER Than It Was During The Dotcom Boom,* Huffpost US, viewed 13 August 2020 <https://www.huffingtonpost.co.uk/entry/start-up-activity-higher_n_590403?ri18n=true&guccounter=1&guce_referrer=aHR0cHM6Ly93d3cuZ29vZ2xlLmNvbS88&guce_referrer_

sig=AQAAALWi7waFCvavz2RyavZHgjMjAMt3fsKvWF_br4_
OSX0UxkyrbuHi_YE17cdgWTHc8F01O3JCGsyyEPc1vHwjH_
VXy_BcssQRHXINs8r-Od2jPr4pM015kaORG0OJ0m99Difd2g
cKYJG6rL0Fti5433CvTJKEQrQMw3WYaWKKRdyo>

20. Card, J, 2017, *Financial crises are a 'filtering mechanism' for start-ups*, The Guardian, viewed 13 August 2020 <https://www.theguardian.com/small-business-network/2017/jan/24/financial-crises-filtering-mechanism-startups>

21. Card, J, 2017, *Financial crises are a 'filtering mechanism' for start-ups*, The Guardian, viewed 13 August 2020 <https://www.theguardian.com/small-business-network/2017/jan/24/financial-crises-filtering-mechanism-startups>

22. Card, J, 2017, *Financial crises are a 'filtering mechanism' for start-ups*, The Guardian, viewed 13 August 2020 <https://www.theguardian.com/small-business-network/2017/jan/24/financial-crises-filtering-mechanism-startups>

23. Warren, K, 2020, *Airbnb has laid of 25% of its staff. Meet CEO Brian Chesky, who cofounded the company in 2008 to help pay his San Francisco apartment's rent and is now worth $4.1 billion*, Business Insider, viewed 13 August 2020 <https://www.businessinsider.com/brian-chesky-airbnb-life-career-net-worth-relationship-philanthropy?r=US&IR=T#:~:text=Brian%20Chesky%2C%20the%20CEO%20and,event%20in%20the%20Nevada%20desert.>

24. Conklin, A, 2020, *10 successful startups founded during 2008 Great Recession*, Fox Business, viewed 13 August 2020 <https://www.foxbusiness.com/markets/startups-great-recession>

25. Conklin, A, 2020, *10 successful startups founded during 2008 Great Recession*, Fox Business, viewed 13 August 2020 <https://www.foxbusiness.com/markets/startups-great-recession>

26. Business Wire, 2020, *Intuit to Acquire Credit Karma*, viewed 13 August 2020 <https://www.businesswire.com/news/home/20200224005884/en/Intuit-Acquire-Credit-Karma>

27. Conklin, A, 2020, *10 successful startups founded during 2008 Great Recession*, Yahoo News, viewed 13 August 2020 <https://www.foxbusiness.com/markets/startups-great-recession>

28. Thompson, L, 2020, *Meet the people who have launched exciting new businesses in lockdown,* Metro News, viewed 13 August 2020 <https://metro.co.uk/2020/07/14/meet-people-who-have-launched-exciting-new-businesses-lockdown-12983610/>

29. Thompson, L, 2020, *Meet the people who have launched exciting new businesses in lockdown,* Metro News, viewed 13 August 2020 <https://metro.co.uk/2020/07/14/meet-people-who-have-launched-exciting-new-businesses-lockdown-12983610/>

30. Williams, A, 2020, *'I started a business during lockdown': meet the entrepreneurs profiting in a pandemic,* The Telegraph, viewed 13 August 2020 <https://www.telegraph.co.uk/money/consumer-affairs/started-business-lockdown-meet-entrepreneurs-profiting-pandemic/>

31. Williams, A, 2020, *'I started a business during lockdown': meet the entrepreneurs profiting in a pandemic,* The Telegraph, viewed 13 August 2020 <https://www.telegraph.co.uk/money/consumer-affairs/started-business-lockdown-meet-entrepreneurs-profiting-pandemic/>

32. Goodreads.com, 2020, *Joseph Campbell Quotable Quotes,* viewed 13 August 2020 <https://www.goodreads.com/quotes/230531-opportunities-to-find-deeper-powers-within-ourselves-come-when-life>

33. AZ Quotes, 2020, *Alvin Toffler Quotes,* viewed 13 August 2020 <https://www.azquotes.com/quote/295333>

34. Anderson, C, 2013, *Jay Abraham Quotes,* Smart Busines Trends, viewed 13 August 2020 <https://smartbusinesstrends.com/jay-abraham-quotes/>

35. Hansen, MV, 2020, *Mark Victor Hansen,* Goodreads.com, viewed 13 August 2020 <https://www.goodreads.com/author/show/25217.Mark_Victor_Hansen>

36. Hightower, C, 2020, *14 Cullen Hightower Quotes,* Brainy Quote, viewed 13 August 2020 <https://www.brainyquote.com/authors/cullen-hightower-quotes>

    Harvey S. Firestone title quote: Find Your Nerve, 2013, *Find Your Nerve,* McKee Wallwork & Company LLC, viewed 13 August 2020 <http://findyournerve.com/fact_is>

37. Tracy, B, 2020, *A major stimulant to creative thinking is focuses questions,* Quotefancy, viewed 13 August 2020 <https://quotefancy.com/quote/778248/Brian-Tracy-A-major-stimulant-to-creative-thinking-is-focused-questions-There-is>

38. Stewart, M, 2020, *Quotes by Martha Stewart,* What Should I Read Next, viewed 13 August 2020 <https://www.whatshouldireadnext.com/quotes/martha-stewart-i-m-not-a-sponge-exactly>

39. Eisner, M, 2020, *Michael Eisner Quotes,* Brainy Quote, viewed 13 August 2020 <https://www.brainyquote.com/authors/michael-eisner-quotes>

40. PWC UK, 2015, *A New Urban Agenda: Accommodating 2 billion new urban citizens,* viewed 13 August 2020 <https://www.pwc.co.uk/issues/megatrends/rapid-urbanisation.html>

41. Mintel, 2020 *Global Consumer Trends 2030,* Mintel Group, viewed 13 August 2020 <https://www.mintel.com/global-consumer-trends?gclid=EAIaIQobChMInfCB2IOU6wIViLbtCh0DZwhFEAAYASAAEgLmyPD_BwE>

42. The International Journal of Newspaper Technology, 2020 *Newspaper Ovation,* viewed 13 August 2020 <http://www.newsandtecharchives.com/ovation/ovation.htm>

43. Branson, R, 2020, *Richard Branson Quotes,* Brainy Quote, viewed 13 August 2020 <https://www.brainyquote.com/authors/richard-branson-quotes>

44. Walker, CJ, 2020, *C.J. Walker,* Goodreads.com, viewed 13 August 2020 <https://www.goodreads.com/author/show/3378102.C_J_Walker>

45. Bushnell, B, 2020, *Nolan Bushnell,* Goodreads.com, viewed 13 August 2020 <https://www.goodreads.com/author/show/2922149.Nolan_Bushnell>

46. Reportlinker.com, 2019, *Global Interior Design Industry,* Globe News Wire, viewed 13 August 2020 <https://www.globenewswire.com/news-release/2019/10/14/1929013/0/en/Global-Interior-Design-Industry.html>

47. Low, E, 2020, *Animation Production Charges Ahead as Pandemic Halts the Rest of Entertainment Industry,* Variety, viewed 13 August 2020 <https://variety.com/2020/tv/news/animation-production-remote-coronavirus-pandemic-1234616856/>

48. Supplee, S, 2020, *Home* [Pinterest post], Pinterest, viewed 13 August 2020 <https://www.pinterest.co.uk/pin/414331234467168711/?autologin=true>

49. Kalantri, A, 2020, *Amit Kalantri,* Goodreads.com, viewed 13 August 2020 <https://www.goodreads.com/author/show/6590179.Amit_Kalantri>

50. Berger, T, 2020, *Thomas Berger Quotes,* Brainy Quote, viewed 13 August 2020 <https://www.brainyquote.com/authors/thomas-berger-quotes>

51. Quillen, R, 2020, *Robert Quillen Quotes,* Brainy Quote, viewed 13 August 2020 <https://www.brainyquote.com/authors/robert-quillen-quotes>

52. Supplee, S, 2020, *Home* [Pinterest post], Pinterest, viewed 13 August 2020 <https://nl.pinterest.com/pin/414331234466971979/?amp_client_id=CLIENT_ID(_)&mweb_unauth_id=&simplified=true>

53. Berra, LP, 2020, *Yogi Berra,* Goodreads.com, viewed 13 August 2020 <https://www.goodreads.com/author/show/79014.Yogi_Berra>

Grenville Main title quote: Schmidt, N, 2013, *Marketing Part Two: Brands,* Words & Pictures, viewed 13 August 2020 <https://www.wordsandpics.org/2013/06/marketing-part-two-brands.html>

54. Biz Community, 2008, *Marketing Quotes South Africa,* viewed 13 August 2020 <https://www.bizcommunity.com/Quote/196/423/2651.html>

55. Neville, 2006, *Karen Katz – Neiman Marcus and Randall Pinkett,* NevBlog, viewed 13 August 2020 <https://www.nevblog.com/karen-katz-neiman-marcus-and-randal-pinkett/>

56. Biz Community, 2007, *Retail Service Quotes South Africa,* viewed 13 August 2020 <https://www.bizcommunity.com/Quote/196/188/2406.html>

57. Ackerman, D, 2020, *Diane Ackerman Quotes,* Citatis, viewed 13 August 2020 <https://citatis.com/a39315/>

58. Eisner, M, 2015, *Michael Eisner Quotes,* AZ Quotes, viewed 13 August 2020 <https://www.azquotes.com/author/4408-Michael_Eisner>

    Rudy Giuliani title quote: The New York Times, 2012, *Giuliani's Speech at the Republican National Convention,* viewed 13 August 2020 <https://www.nytimes.com/elections/2008/president/conventions/videos/transcripts/20080903_giuliani_speech.html>

    Michael Porter title quote: Hammonds, K, 2001, *Michael Porter's Big Ideas,* Fast Company, viewed 13 August 2020 <https://www.fastcompany.com/42485/michael-porters-big-ideas>

59. Burnett, L, 2020, *Leo Burnett Quotes,* Brainy Quotes, viewed 13 August 2020 <https://www.brainyquote.com/authors/leo-burnett-quotes>

60. Daye, D, 2010, *The Advertising Wisdom of Bill Bernbach,* Business Strategy Insider, viewed 13 August 2020 <https://www.brandingstrategyinsider.com/the-advertising-wisdom-of-bill-bernbach/#.XzMWcShKg2w>

61. Lec, SJ, 2020, *Stanislaw Jerzy Lec Quotes,* Brainy Quotes, viewed 13 August 2020 <https://www.brainyquote.com/authors/stanislaw-jerzy-lec-quotes>

62. Zarlenga, PN, 2020 *Peter Nivio Zarlenga Quotes,* Brainy Quotes, viewed 13 August 2020 <https://www.brainyquote.com/authors/peter-nivio-zarlenga-quotes>

63. Ogilvy, D, 2020 *David Ogilvy Quotes,* Brainy Quotes, viewed 13 August 2020 <https://www.brainyquote.com/authors/david-ogilvy-quotes>

64. Richards, JI, 2020, *Jef I Richards Quotes,* Brainy Quotes, viewed 13 August 2020 <https://www.brainyquote.com/authors/jef-i-richards-quotes>

65. Neville, 2006, *Karen Katz – Neiman Marcus and Randall Pinkett,* NevBlog, viewed 13 August 2020 <https://www.nevblog.com/karen-katz-neiman-marcus-and-randal-pinkett/>

66. Kemp, S, 2019, *Global Social Media Users Pass 3.5 Billion,* We Are Social, viewed 13 August 2020 <https://wearesocial.com/blog/2019/07/global-social-media-users-pass-3-5-billion>

67. Fast Marketing Plan, 2018, *Famous Quotes About Plans and Planning,* viewed 13 August 2020 <http://www.fastmarketingplan.com/tips/famous-quotes-about-plans-planning.php>

68. Corrigan, C, 2020, *You can't overestimate the ned to plan and prepare,* Quotefancy, viewed 13 August 2020 <https://quotefancy.com/quote/1580782/Chris-Corrigan-You-can-t-overestimate-the-need-to-plan-and-prepare-In-most-of-the>

69. Schuller, RH, 2020, *Robert H Schuller Quotes,* Brainy Quote, viewed 13 August 2020 <https://www.brainyquote.com/authors/robert-h-schuller-quotes>

70. Sinclair, S, 2011, *You are the embodiment of the information you choose to accept and act upon,* Positively Positive, viewed 13 August 2020 <https://www.positivelypositive.com/quotes/you-are-the-embodiment-of-the-information-you-choose-to-accept-and-act-upon-to-change-your-circumstances-you-need-to-change-your-thinking-and-subsequent-actions/>

71. Hoffer, E, 2020, *Eric Hoffer Quotes,* Brainy Quote, viewed 13 August 2020 <https://www.brainyquote.com/authors/eric-hoffer-quotes>

72. Hill, N, 2020, *Napoleon Hill Quotes,* Brainy Quotes, viewed 13 August 2020 <https://www.brainyquote.com/authors/napoleon-hill-quotes>

73. Maxwell, JC, 2020, *John C Maxwell Quotes,* Brainy Quote, viewed 13 August 2020 <https://www.brainyquote.com/authors/john-c-maxwell-quotes>

74. Maxwell, JC, 2020, *John C Maxwell Quotes,* Brainy Quote, viewed 13 August 2020 <https://www.brainyquote.com/authors/john-c-maxwell-quotes>

75. Marston, R, 2020, *Ralph Marston Quotes,* Brainy Quote, viewed 13 August 2020 <https://www.brainyquote.com/authors/ralph-marston-quotes>

References | 191

76. Galer, G, 2020, *Integrity is what we do, what we say, and what we say we do,* Quotegeek, viewed 13 August 2020 <http://quotegeek.com/literature/don-galer/3176/>

77. Fuller, RB, 2020, *R. Buckminster Fuller Quotes,* Brainy Quote, viewed 13 August 2020 <https://www.brainyquote.com/authors/r-buckminster-fuller-quotes>

78. Baker, H, 2020, *Howard Baker Quotes,* Brainy Quote, viewed 13 August 2020 <https://www.brainyquote.com/authors/howard-baker-quotes>

79. Drucker, P, 2020, *Peter Drucker Quotes,* viewed 13 August 2020 <https://www.brainyquote.com/authors/peter-drucker-quotes>

80. Schattke, J, 2020, *Necessity is the mother of invension,* FinestQuotes.com, viewed 13 August 2020 <http://www.finestquotes.com/quote-id-27567.htm>

81. Koslow, B, 2020, *The freedom to move forward to new opportunities and to produce results comes from living in the present, not the past,* Power Quotations, viewed 13 August 2020 <https://www.powerquotations.com/quote/the-freedom-to-move-forward>

82. Cook, ML, 2007, *Mary Lou Cook,* Goodreads.com <https://www.goodreads.com/author/show/761062.Mary_Lou_Cook>

83. Allen, W, 2020, *Inspirational Quotations,* Rightattitudes.com, viewed 13 August 2020 <http://www.inspiration.rightattitudes.com/authors/woody-allen/>

OTHER PUBLICATIONS

  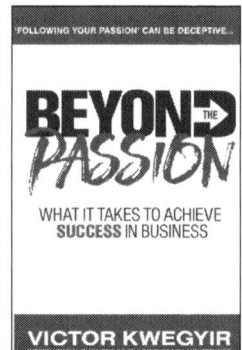

AVAILABLE WORLDWIDE

For business coaching or help to publish your book, contact us via:
admin@victorkwegyir.com | admin@vikesprings.com

Connect with author:

 /victorkwegyir   /victorkwegyir   /victorkwegyir   @vikek

Websites: admin@victorkwegyir.com   admin@vikesprings.com

Printed in Great Britain
by Amazon